Eagles Mere Inn

Box #356 Eagles Mere PA 17731

(717) 525-3273   (800) 426-3273

COUNTRY INNS
AND BACK ROADS
COOKBOOK

Country Inns and Back Roads Cookbook

NEW EDITION

Linda Glick Conway

BERKSHIRE HOUSE PUBLISHERS
Stockbridge, Massachusetts

Country Inns and Back Roads Cookbook
Copyright © 1995 by Berkshire House Publishers
Interior photographs © 1995 by Craig Hammell and other credited sources

Photography and photo editing by Craig Hammell
Cover illustration, cover design, and text design and layout by Pamela Meier
Production services by Ripinsky & Company

Library of Congress Cataloging-in-Publication Data

Conway, Linda Glick.
Country inns and back roads cookbook / Linda Glick Conway.—New ed.
        p.   cm.
ISBN 0-936399-69-4
1. Cookery, American. 2. Cookery, Canadian. 3. Hotels—United States.
4. Hotels—Canada, Eastern. I. Title.
TX715.C75892   1995
641.5973—dc20   95-12024

ISBN 0-936399-69-4

10 9 8 7 6 5 4 3 2 1
Printed in the United States of America

Contents

To my mother, Virginia Pearce Glick,
who introduced me to the byways

Foreword

What makes a country inn special and its food a particular delight? I remember my own first visit to a country inn as an adult, when in the late 1960s a friend and I drove from Boston to Newfane, Vermont, for a midweek escape from our labors in the mines of book publishing. We couldn't have been more pleased. The village was lovely (and still is), the inn combined the feel of Grandmother's house with the sophistication of a French *auberge*, the sitting room bookshelves were full of enticing volumes, and, perhaps most important, dinner and breakfast were delectable. We were able to ski nearby (until lack of skill wore us out), and there were enough antiques shops in the area to satisfy our burgeoning habit.

All these years later my motives and, I suspect, those of most country inn habitués, are the same. We are in search of a place that seems like home but isn't, where the hosts seem like family but aren't, and the cooking is not only as good as Mother's but better. We hope for features and facilities that allow us to indulge our favorite activities—sports, fitness, reading, shopping, scenic drives—whatever those may be. Most of all, we want to eat well—to enjoy the specialties of the region and try interesting new preparations.

Norman Simpson, originator of the Country Inns and Back Roads travel guides, decided as early as 1968 to celebrate the special cooking that takes place in country inns with the publication of *The Country Inn Cookbook*. This book went through several printings, and other cookbooks followed. His best-known title, *Country Inns and Back Roads Cookbook*, first appeared in 1980; it has remained in print continuously, and now, fifteen years later, we are launching an entirely new edition. Though exactly half the inns included in this book were in the 1980 book, many of the establishments represented here were not in operation in 1980. From old inns or new, the recipes in this collection are all new.

Though *Country Inns and Back Roads Cookbook* is mainly for cooks, armchair or actual, it may also serve the traveler. I have tried to provide the "flavor" of the inns, if not all the pertinent details. The establishments included in the book have been recognized in ways too numerous to mention on an individual basis—they have won countless awards, been the subject of numerous magazine pieces, occupy buildings listed on the National Register of Historic Places, and employ chefs trained at the most prestigious culinary institutes. For complete information, contact the inns directly, using the list of Inns and Their Addresses that follows the text.

In addition to the innkeepers and chefs, who contributed so generously of their time and talents, I would like to thank Jean Rousseau, publisher of Berkshire House, who first suggested the idea of updating Norman Simpson's classic volume. I am indebted to his staff—Madeleine Gruen, Philip Rich, and Mary Osak—as well as to Cornelia Parkinson, copyeditor, and Constance Oxley, proofreader. Special thanks are owed to Georgeanne Rousseau, who volunteered to read the manuscript and made many helpful suggestions. Finally, my husband and office mate, Jim Conway, is always supportive of my work. I thank him for that and for sharing my love of country inns and good food.

As a practical word to the cooks who use this book, I should mention that all eggs called for are large, and vegetables are medium unless otherwise indicated. Temperatures given are for standard, not convection, ovens. With the exception of procedures for roasting red peppers, clarifying butter, and preparing a roux, the instructions are from the inns' chefs, which means the same procedure may be handled differently from one recipe to another.

Whatever your purpose, enjoy browsing, cooking, or just plain dreaming.

Linda Glick Conway
August 1995

COUNTRY INNS
AND BACK ROADS
COOKBOOK

Appetizers

Appetizers

Mussels Dijon
Chilled Sesame Ginger Mussels
Cassolette d'Escargots
Escargots à la Brandi
Orange Spice Shrimp
Scallops with Roasted Red Pepper, Leeks, and Lemon Butter
Smoked Seafood Mousse
Salmon Tartare with Nut Oil and Cilantro
Salmon Cakes
Paul's Excellent Crab Cakes with Corn Relish
Crabmeat Quesadillas
Liver Pâté
Grilled Duck Breast and Prosciutto Terrine with Cranberry Purée
Terrine of Grilled Vegetables and Goat Cheese
Honeyed Salad of Wild Mushrooms with Hatley Goat Cheese
Grilled Portabella Mushrooms
Stuffed Mushroom Appetizer
Rillettes of Goose in White Wine
Camembert Crisp with Gooseberry Chutney and Croûtons
Appetizer Pizza
The Wickwood Summer Tart
Spinach and Chèvre Tarts

Mussels Dijon

THE VERMONT INN, KILLINGTON, VERMONT

The emphasis on gourmet cooking at the Vermont Inn is obvious—Susan and Judd Levy's brochure includes a complete dinner menu, sure to make the decision to stay at their converted 1840s farmhouse an easy one. Down the road from Killington, billed as New England's largest ski area, the inn offers a cozy respite from the madding crowds.

2 dozen mussels
1 tablespoon olive oil
1 tablespoon minced garlic
1/4 cup sliced Spanish onion
1/4 cup white wine
1 tablespoon Dijon mustard
1/2 cup heavy cream
1/2 cup bottled clam juice

1. Debeard and scrub the mussels.

2. Heat a large sauté pan, place the oil in the pan, and sauté the garlic and onions until soft. Deglaze the pan with the white wine over medium high heat, add the mustard, and stir to combine.

3. Place the mussels, cream, and clam juice in the pan. Cover with a second pan (inverted) to create a steamer. Lower the heat slightly and steam for 5 minutes. The mussels are done when the shells open and the mussels are firm.

4. Heap the mussels in a large bowl and pour the broth over them. Serve with crusty bread for dipping.

Serves 2.

Note: For a lighter version, skim milk may be used in place of the heavy cream.

Chilled Sesame Ginger Mussels

PILGRIM'S INN, DEER ISLE, MAINE

Considering the fairly recent proliferation of country inns, Jean and Dud Hendrick's fourteen years at Pilgrim's Inn seems a venerable record. Their imposing eighteenth-century house was built in 1793 by Ignatius Haskell, Esquire, and it was his daughter, Rebeccah, who first began to offer rest and relaxation to the traveler. Deer Isle is beautifully situated in Penobscot Bay, home to some of the best sailing in North America.

2 dozen mussels, debearded and cleaned
1 cup white wine
2 tablespoons minced fresh ginger root
1/2 cup soy sauce
1 teaspoon sesame oil
1 teaspoon red wine vinegar
1 teaspoon sugar
1 tablespoon minced fresh cilantro
1 small red onion, chopped
1 tablespoon dry mustard

1. Cook the mussels, wine, and 1 tablespoon of the ginger in a large covered stainless steel pot over medium heat until the shells open, about 5 minutes. Remove from heat and let cool.

2. Remove the mussels from the shells, place them in a stainless steel bowl, and reserve the shells.

3. Combine the remaining ingredients in the bowl of a food processor and process for 10 seconds. Pour the mixture over the mussels and allow to sit at room temperature for 1 hour.

4. To serve, divide the mussels and some of the marinade among the reserved shells. Serve six per person.

Serves 4.

Cassolette d'Escargots

THE HOMESTEAD INN, GREENWICH, CONNECTICUT

*In a sophisticated town adjacent to metropolitan New York City, expect the
unexpected—a tranquil 23-room inn set among shade trees and rolling lawns.
The main building is a 1799 farmhouse completely restored in 1979 by owners
Lessie Davison and Nancy Smith. An important part of the complex is
LaGrange restaurant, once a barn and now home to the fine cuisine of French
chef Jacques Thiebeult, formerly of New York restaurants Le Cirque and Le
Cygne. Here is one of his most popular recipes, not only because it tastes delicious
but because it eliminates the need to struggle with shells and tongs.*

1 tablespoon butter
24 escargots (snails)
5 ounces chanterelle mushrooms
2 teaspoons chopped shallots
4 tablespoons garlic butter (softened butter mixed with small amounts
   of minced garlic, shallots, parsley, and salt and pepper to taste)
1/2 cup heavy cream
1/2 teaspoon (a splash) Pernod liqueur (optional)
Chopped parsley, for garnish

1. Heat the butter in a sauté pan and add the snails, mushrooms, and
   shallots. Sauté until the mushrooms just begin to give off their juices,
   making sure that the shallots do not burn.

2. Add the garlic butter and swirl until it melts. Add the cream and
   Pernod and cook until the mixture reduces somewhat.

3. Divide the mixture among four individual casseroles, sprinkle with the
   chopped parsley, and serve immediately.

Serves 4.

Escargots à la Brandi

SCHUMACHER'S NEW PRAGUE HOTEL, NEW PRAGUE, MINNESOTA

Twenty-five minutes south of the Twin Cities, one can step into another world in the aptly named town of New Prague, where the citizens' Czech heritage is perhaps best represented in the ever-expanding business of John and Kathleen Schumacher. According to one review, their New Prague Hotel is a slice of European graciousness in the heart of the Midwest. The décor, the hospitality, and the cuisine all reflect the warmth and charm of a Central European inn. The following dish is named for Chef John's daughter Brandi.

16 large mushroom caps, washed, dried, and stems removed

1 cup (2 sticks) butter or margarine, at room temperature

4 slices bacon, cooked, drained, and crumbled

2 tablespoons minced shallots

1 tablespoon chopped parsley

4 cloves garlic, minced, or 1½ teaspoons garlic powder

2 tablespoons Cognac

16 bay scallops

16 escargots (snails)

8 toast points (4 slices bread, toasted and cut on the diagonal)

1. Preheat the oven to 350 degrees F. Grease a small baking pan.

2. Place the mushroom caps in the prepared pan, hollow sides up.

3. Stir the butter to lighten, and add the bacon, shallots, parsley, garlic, and Cognac. Combine well.

4. Place ½ teaspoon of the butter mixture in each mushroom cap and top with 1 scallop and 1 snail. Cover each with a rounded teaspoon of the butter mixture.

5. Bake for 20 to 25 minutes, or until golden brown. Serve on individual plates, with toast points.

Serves 4.

Orange Spice Shrimp

THE BIRD & BOTTLE INN, GARRISON, NEW YORK

A former stagecoach stop on the Old Albany Post Road, this lovely inn has been operating as The Bird & Bottle since 1940. Under the current ownership of Ira Boyar, it is a sophisticated hostelry noted for its culinary prowess.

4 cups freshly squeezed orange juice
4 tablespoons hot sauce
2 tablespoons light brown sugar
2 tablespoons Worcestershire sauce
1 tablespoon minced garlic
36 jumbo shrimp, peeled and deveined

1. Place all the ingredients except the shrimp in a large frying pan. Bring to a boil, reduce the heat, and simmer for 5 minutes.

2. Add the shrimp to the pan and cook for 4 minutes, or until they are pink and firm.

3. Heat six individual serving plates, place the shrimp on the plates, and set aside.

4. Reduce the sauce over high heat for 2 to 3 minutes and pour over the shrimp. Serve immediately.

Serves 6.

Scallops with Roasted Red Pepper, Leeks, and Lemon Butter

NATHANIEL PORTER INN, WARREN, RHODE ISLAND

Robert Lynch, who owns the Nathaniel Porter Inn with his wife, Paulette, saved the handsome Georgian mansion from the wrecking ball in 1981. An old-house buff, he also wanted to make a contribution to the community his grandmother had settled in as an emigrant from Poland in 1905.

1/4 cup canola oil

3/4 pound scallops

2 leeks, white part only, cleaned and sliced

3 red bell peppers, roasted, peeled, seeded, and sliced (see note page 13)

Juice of 1 lemon

1/4 cup white wine (optional)

2 tablespoons butter

Salt and freshly ground pepper to taste

7 tablespoons chopped fresh dill

1. Heat the oil in a frying pan over high heat. Add the scallops and sauté, turning, until lightly brown.

2. Add the leeks and strips of red pepper and cook until the leeks are soft.

3. Add the lemon juice and wine. Lower the heat, cook to reduce the liquid slightly, then add the butter, a little at a time, swirling between additions. Season with salt and pepper.

4. Stir in the dill and serve immediately on individual plates.

Serves 4.

Smoked Seafood Mousse

THE INN ON THE COMMON, CRAFTSBURY COMMON, VERMONT

Vermont's Northeast Kingdom has a personality of its own, and Craftsbury Common may well be its most picturesque village. It is a true hill town, and the Inn on the Common occupies fifteen of its loveliest hilltop acres, with breathtaking views of the Green Mountains. Owners Penny and Michael Schmitt have spent many years honing their innkeeping skills, and the attention to detail is notable in every aspect of one's stay—comfort, décor, ambience, and, of course, food.

1 envelope unflavored gelatin

1/4 cup cold water

1/2 cup boiling water

1/3 cup mayonnaise or plain yogurt

3 tablespoons chopped fresh dill

1 tablespoon grated onion

1/2 tablespoon fresh lemon juice

1/2 tablespoon fresh lime juice

1/4 teaspoon cayenne pepper

1/4 teaspoon paprika

1 cup flaked smoked trout

1 cup finely chopped smoked shrimp

1 cup heavy cream

1. Soften the gelatin in the cold water in a large bowl. Add the boiling water and stir until the gelatin is dissolved. Add the mayonnaise, dill, onion, lemon and lime juices, cayenne, and paprika and whisk to combine well.

2. Pour half the gelatin mixture into a separate bowl. Fold the smoked trout into half of the mixture and the smoked shrimp into the other half.

3. Whip the cream until stiff peaks form and fold half into each seafood mixture. Layer the mixture in individual glasses or glass dishes or in a large bowl. Chill, covered, overnight.

4. Serve with crackers or raw vegetables.

Serves 8 to 10.

Note: Any smoked seafood may be substituted for the trout or shrimp.

Salmon Tartare with Nut Oil and Cilantro

BLANTYRE, LENOX, MASSACHUSETTS

A classic Berkshire Cottage fallen into disrepair, Blantyre was purchased by the Fitzpatrick family in 1980 and opened three years later as one of America's finest country house hotels. The Tudor-style mansion, a replica of a grand Scottish manor house, sits amid 85 acres of spectacular rolling countryside. Eight bedrooms and suites in the main house, distinctively decorated with lush fabrics and antiques, are supplemented by twelve similar accommodations in the nearby Carriage House.

3 pearl onions, minced

3 shallots, minced

1 small clove garlic, minced

1 cup cold water

1 pound raw salmon, cut in 1/4-inch dice

2 tablespoons Thai fish sauce

1 tablespoon walnut oil

1 tablespoon hazelnut oil

5 tablespoons extra virgin olive oil

2 teaspoons chopped fresh dill

2 teaspoons chopped fresh cilantro

1 European cucumber, peeled, thinly sliced, and lightly salted

1/2 cup crème fraîche

Olive Oil-Lemon Dressing (see recipe below)

Dill sprigs, for garnish

1. Place the onions, shallots, garlic, and water in a small saucepan and bring to a boil over medium heat. Drain the vegetables and let cool.

2. In a bowl, combine the salmon, fish sauce, oils, dill, and cilantro and mix well. Add the cooled vegetables and mix again.

3. Place the cucumber circles in a 4-inch circle in the center of six salad plates.

4. Oil a 3-inch biscuit cutter and pack it with the salmon mixture. Unmold on top of the cucumbers. Repeat five times.

5. Top the salmon with a thin layer of crème fraîche and drizzle the Olive Oil-Lemon Dressing around the edge. Garnish each serving with a sprig of dill.

Serves 6.

Olive Oil-Lemon Dressing

1/4 cup olive oil
1 tablespoon fresh lemon juice
1 teaspoon sugar
Salt and freshly ground pepper to taste

Combine all the ingredients in a small bowl and whisk to blend.

Salmon Cakes

THE INN AT THORN HILL, JACKSON, NEW HAMPSHIRE

The noted architect Stanford White designed what is now the main house at the Inn at Thorn Hill in 1895. Victorian furnishings and décor extend throughout, with Mt. Washington and lesser White Mountains visible from many rooms. Also on the property are a carriage house with a country ambience, suitable for conferences and groups traveling together, and three cottages for individuals or small families.

1 cup mayonnaise, preferably homemade

2 red bell peppers, roasted, peeled, and minced

2 tablespoons drained capers, minced

2 pounds fresh salmon fillet, skinned

1/2 cup minced onion

2 eggs, lightly beaten

2 teaspoons fresh lemon juice

1/2 cup bread crumbs

4 teaspoons Dijon mustard

1 teaspoon salt

1/2 teaspoon cayenne pepper

Cornmeal, for dredging

Oil and butter, for sautéing

Mixed greens or watercress, for garnish

1. Place the mayonnaise in the bowl of a food processor, add 1/2 cup of the minced roasted pepper and process until the pepper has been puréed.

2. Set aside 1/2 cup of the mayonnaise-pepper purée. Add the capers to the remaining purée, to create a rémoulade sauce (for a spicier sauce, add some minced jalapeño pepper). Set aside.

3. Cut the salmon into 1-inch pieces and coarsely chop in a food processor.

4. Transfer the mixture to a bowl and add the onion, the remaining minced roasted pepper, eggs, lemon juice, bread crumbs, mustard, salt, and cayenne. Blend in the 1/2 cup set-aside mayonnaise-pepper purée and mix well. Chill the mixture.

5. Shape the salmon mixture into 12 patties, dredge in cornmeal and sauté in a mixture of butter and oil until brown on both sides.

6. Serve with a dollop of rémoulade and garnish with mixed greens or watercress.

Serves 6.

Note: To roast peppers, spear with a fork and char over the flame of a gas burner until completely blackened. Place in a plastic bag, seal the bag, and let the peppers cool. When cool, the skins will be loose and easy to peel away. Remove the skins and seeds and use as directed.

Paul's Excellent Crab Cakes with Corn Relish

THE INN AT MONTPELIER, MONTPELIER, VERMONT

One of the prides of Vermont's capital city is the New England Culinary Institute, and the Inn at Montpelier is blessed to have one of its graduates, Paul Hoffert, as chef. His crab cakes are a popular appetizer in the inn's two intimate dining rooms.

1 tablespoon butter

1/2 onion, finely diced

1 celery stalk, diced

1/2 teaspoon dried thyme

1/2 teaspoon ground cumin

Pinch of cayenne pepper

1 tablespoon all-purpose flour

1/4 cup dry bread crumbs

1/2 cup light cream

1 egg, lightly beaten

1 tablespoon dry mustard

1 pound Maine crabmeat, well picked over

Flour, cornmeal, or dry bread crumbs, for dredging

Butter, for sautéing

Corn Relish (see recipe below)

1. Heat the butter in a sauté pan and add the onion, celery, thyme, cumin, and cayenne. Sauté until the onion is translucent, 8 to 10 minutes.

2. Add the flour, bread crumbs, and cream. Bring to a simmer and cook for 5 minutes. Remove from the heat and allow to cool for 10 minutes.

3. Add the egg and mustard and mix well. Cool completely and add the crabmeat.

4. Chill the crabmeat mixture, shape into patties, roll in flour, cornmeal, or dry bread crumbs and sauté in butter until brown on both sides. Serve with Corn Relish.

Serves 4.

Corn Relish

8 ears corn
1/2 cup water
1 cup cider vinegar
3/4 cup sugar
1 1/2 teaspoons salt
1 tablespoon mustard seed
1/2 teaspoon celery seed
1 tablespoon dry mustard
1 1/2 teaspoons cornstarch
1 red bell pepper, diced
1 green bell pepper, diced
1/2 large onion, diced

1. Cook the corn on the cob and slice off the kernels (you should have about 4 cups). Set aside.

2. Combine the water, vinegar, sugar, salt, mustard seed, celery seed, dry mustard, and cornstarch in a saucepan. Bring to a boil over medium heat and add the peppers and onion. Simmer for 10 minutes, stirring occasionally.

3. Stir in the corn and cook for 5 more minutes. Cool and spoon into one or two jars. The relish will keep, covered, in the refrigerator for two to three weeks.

Makes about 4 cups.

Note: If you wish to have more relish on hand or to can it for future use (using sterilized canning methods), the recipe may be doubled.

Crabmeat Quesadillas

MURPHIN RIDGE INN, WEST UNION, OHIO

Bob and Mary Crosset, former Cincinnati schoolteachers, have opted for a more peaceful setting in a small town fifty miles east of the city. Their current home consists of an 1810 farmhouse, where the highly praised meals at Murphin Ridge Inn are served, and a barnlike building erected in 1990 (with the help of the local Amish community) that houses the inn's guest rooms. The property's more than 700 acres include a swimming pool, tennis court, hiking trails, and ample space for lawn games.

16 6-inch flour tortillas
1 cup grated Monterey Jack cheese
2 cups fresh crabmeat, picked over and lightly shredded
1 cup grated jalapeño pepper cheese
2 tablespoons chopped fresh cilantro
Vegetable oil
Sour cream, for garnish
Minced scallions, for garnish

1. Preheat the oven to 400 degrees F.

2. Lay eight of the tortillas on a work surface. Divide the Monterey jack cheese evenly among the tortillas, spreading to the edges of each one.

3. Spread the crabmeat over the Jack cheese. Repeat with the pepper cheese.

4. Sprinkle each tortilla with the cilantro and top with the remaining eight tortillas. Press down firmly to flatten.

5. Brush a thin film of oil on the top of each tortilla sandwich and place on a sheet pan. Bake just until the cheese melts, 8 to 10 minutes, then place under a broiler for approximately 10 seconds, just until the tops begin to brown.

6. Cut into sixths and serve immediately, garnished with a dollop of sour cream and a sprinkling of scallions.

Serves 8.

Liver Pâté

THE HANCOCK INN, HANCOCK, NEW HAMPSHIRE

The oldest inn in New Hampshire in continuous operation has long had a reputation for fine food, beginning with mid-nineteenth-century innkeeper David Patten, known as Squire Patten. He personally broiled the steaks that were the specialty of the house, using fifty cords of rock maple a year to fuel the open fire, the only stove available in those days. A far cry from our dependence on the food processor used in this easy recipe—note the surprise ingredient!

3 pounds chicken livers, fat and membrane removed
1/2 cup (1 stick) butter
1/2 teaspoon cayenne pepper
1/2 teaspoon ground nutmeg
1/2 cup crushed fresh pineapple
Chopped red onion, for garnish

1. Place the chicken livers in a saucepan or sauté pan and pour in water to cover. Bring the water to a boil, then reduce the heat and simmer until the chicken livers are still slightly pink (about 3 minutes, being careful not to overcook).

2. Drain the chicken livers and place in the bowl of a food processor with the butter, cayenne, nutmeg, and pineapple. Process until smooth.

3. Transfer the mixture to serving bowls or crocks, cover with plastic wrap, and chill. Garnish with the red onion.

Makes about 3 cups.

Grilled Duck Breast and Prosciutto Terrine with Cranberry Purée

MONTAGUE INN, SAGINAW, MICHIGAN

At the turn of the century, the Grove District of Saginaw was an enclave of distinctive mansions. Today Montague Inn occupies one of those grand houses—a Georgian Revival that retains its period feel and provides the perfect ambience for elegant hospitality.

2 pounds boneless, skinless duck breast, diced

1 tablespoon minced garlic

1 tablespoon dill weed

1 tablespoon salt

1 teaspoon coarsely ground black pepper

1/3 cup chopped red bell pepper

1/4 cup minced scallions

6 ounces prosciutto, diced

18 slices bacon (approximately, to line pan)

Cranberry Purée (see recipe below)

1. Preheat the oven to 375 degrees F.

2. Place the duck, garlic, dill weed, and salt and pepper in the bowl of a food processor and process until chopped fine. Transfer the mixture to a bowl and add the red pepper, scallions, and prosciutto. Blend well.

3. Line a 12-inch terrine pan with the bacon slices, overlapping the strips and leaving the ends hanging over the sides of the pan.

4. Transfer the duck mixture to the terrine, pressing gently to make sure all the corners are filled. Fold over the overhanging bacon strips to cover the mixture.

5. Place the terrine in a water bath and bake for 30 to 40 minutes, until the top feels firm to the touch. Allow to partially cool in the pan before removing to a board or platter. When the terrine is thoroughly cool, cut it into 1/2-inch slices and grill. Serve with Cranberry Purée.

Serves 12.

Cranberry Purée

1 12-ounce bag fresh cranberries
1/2 cup water
3/4 cup sugar
1/2 teaspoon ground cinnamon

1. Place the cranberries and water in a saucepan, bring to a boil, and simmer until the skins have burst and the berries are soft. Transfer the mixture to the bowl of a food processor, add the sugar and cinnamon, and purée until smooth.

2. Strain the mixture through a fine sieve and cool.

Makes 1 1/2 to 2 cups.

Terrine of Grilled Vegetables and Goat Cheese

THE WHITE HART, SALISBURY, CONNECTICUT

The White Hart is noted for its fine restaurants. Breakfast, lunch, and light suppers are served in the Garden Room and the tavern, and Julie's New American Sea Grill is the showcase restaurant for dinner and Sunday brunch. In this dish, Chef Deena Chafetz uses a very simple vinaigrette as the accompaniment because of the intense flavors of the terrine.

2 bunches leeks (about 6 leeks), well cleaned, left long enough to line the bottom and sides of the mold sideways (with overlap), and sliced in half from top to bottom

1 large eggplant, in 1/4-inch lengthwise slices

2 zucchini, in 1/4-inch lengthwise slices

2 red bell peppers, roasted, peeled, seeded, and sliced (see note page 13)

1 pound asparagus

4 cups goat cheese

1/4 cup minced fresh rosemary

Champagne Vinaigrette (see recipe below)

1. Oil a 6- to 8-cup terrine mold.

2. Grill the leeks, eggplant, zucchini, and asparagus until tender.

3. Line the prepared mold with the leeks, leaving enough length to cover the finished terrine.

4. Combine the goat cheese and the rosemary and blend well. Spread a 1/4-inch layer of the cheese mixture over the leeks. Place a layer of eggplant on top of the cheese.

5. Alternate cheese and the remaining vegetables until all are used and the mold is full. Fold the ends of the leeks over to seal the terrine. Chill for several hours.

6. To serve, gently unmold and slice, using a serrated knife. Accompany with Champagne Vinaigrette.

Serves 8 to 10.

Champagne Vinaigrette

1/4 cup imported Champagne vinegar
3/4 cup extra virgin olive oil
Salt and freshly ground pepper to taste

Combine all the ingredients and mix well.

Makes 1 cup.

Honeyed Salad of Wild Mushrooms with Hatley Goat Cheese

HOVEY MANOR, NORTH HATLEY, QUEBEC

The lovely village of North Hatley has strong connections to the United States and remains a sought-after spot for summer residents and tourists. Many of the first settlers were Loyalists who left New England in the years following 1776, and its original summer people were aristocrats and captains of industry from the southern United States, who were renouncing Yankeeland as a summer destination. (Rumor has it that these travelers from the South would draw the blinds of the train windows as they passed through New England.) Hovey Manor is noted for its gourmet cuisine, and this is by far the most popular appetizer on the winter menu.

1 head Boston lettuce

3 ounces Hatley (or other high quality) goat cheese

1 red delicious apple, cored and sliced

1 tablespoon butter, at room temperature

1 red delicious apple, cored and cubed

6 ounces champignons de Paris, coarsely sliced

3 ounces shiitake mushrooms, coarsely sliced

3 ounces portabella mushrooms, coarsely sliced

6 ounces pleurotte mushrooms, coarsely sliced

2 tablespoons chopped scallions

2 tablespoons clover honey

Salt and freshly ground pepper to taste

1. Arrange the lettuce leaves on four salad plates. Divide the goat cheese into four equal portions and place in the center of each bed of lettuce. Arrange the apple slices around the cheese.

2. Melt the butter in a frying pan. Add the cubed apples and sauté until they are soft. Add the mushrooms, shallots, and honey and continue to sauté until the mushrooms begin to wilt. Season with salt and pepper.

3. Arrange the mushrooms over the cheese and lettuce, making sure to drizzle over the pan juices as well. Serve immediately.

Serves 4.

Grilled Portabella Mushrooms

PINE CREST INN, TRYON, NORTH CAROLINA

Located at the center of North Carolina's Hunt Country, Pine Crest Inn began as the private retreat of equestrian Carter Brown in the early 1900s. Many of the property's original buildings remain, including a 200-year-old log cabin, a woodcutter's cottage, and a stone cottage—adding charm to this full-service inn with all the comforts and amenities of the 1990s.

1 pound (2 to 3 large) portabella mushrooms
1/2 cup olive oil
Juice of 1 lemon
2 cloves garlic, minced
1/4 teaspoon minced parsley
1/4 teaspoon dried basil leaves
Salt and freshly ground pepper to taste
Roasted red or yellow bell pepper strips, for garnish (see note page 13)
Parmesan cheese, for garnish

1. Prepare hot coals for grilling.

2. Trim the stems and slice the mushrooms about 1/2 inch thick. Whisk together the olive oil, lemon juice, garlic, herbs, and salt and pepper.

3. Place the mushrooms in a nonreactive (nonaluminum) bowl and pour over the marinade. Toss to coat. Marinate at room temperature for 15 to 20 minutes.

4. Roast the peppers by placing under a broiler or over an open flame to blacken the entire skin. Place the peppers in a paper bag for about 10 minutes to steam. Peel off the outer skin, cut in half, remove the seeds, and slice lengthwise.

5. Shake the excess marinade from the mushroom slices and arrange on a grill over hot coals. Cook for 1 to 2 minutes per side.

6. Transfer to serving plates and garnish with roasted pepper strips; sprinkle with Parmesan cheese.

Serves 4.

Stuffed Mushroom Appetizer

THE DOCTORS INN AT KINGS GRANT, CAPE MAY
COURT HOUSE, NEW JERSEY

*This inn takes its name from at least three of its owners—first, the doctor who
built the Italianate Victorian in 1854; next, longtime owner zoologist Dr.
Florence Wood; and, finally, the present innkeeper, neonatologist Dr. Carolyn
Crawford. Completely redone by Dr. Crawford in 1993, following years of
neglect culminating with the uninvited residency of a group of motorcyclists
who amused themselves by riding their bikes up and down the black walnut
staircases, Doctors Inn is now an elegant Victorian hostelry.*

3 pounds fresh mushrooms, large enough for stuffing
1/2 cup (1 stick) butter
2 pounds sweet Italian sausage
1 onion, chopped
3 stalks celery, chopped
2 tablespoons chopped fresh sage
1/2 cup fresh bread crumbs
3/4 cup freshly grated Romano cheese
Salt and freshly ground pepper to taste
3/4 cup grated Fontina cheese
Dry white wine

1. Preheat the oven to 400 degrees F.

2. Clean the mushrooms and remove and chop the stems.

3. Melt the butter in a large frying pan. Add the sausage, onion, celery,
   and chopped mushroom stems, and sauté until the onion and celery
   are tender and the sausage is cooked through. Drain off the accumulated
   fat and liquid.

4. Let the mixture cool slightly, then fold in the sage, bread crumbs,
   Romano cheese, and salt and pepper.

5. Stuff the mushrooms with the filling mixture, top with the Fontina
   cheese, and place in a baking dish. Pour enough wine into the pan to
   cover the bottom. Bake for about 15 minutes, until the mushrooms
   are cooked through and the cheese has melted and browned.

Makes 35 to 40.

Rillettes of Goose in White Wine

AUBERGE HANDFIELD, ST-MARC-SUR-RICHELIEU, QUEBEC

Innkeeper Conrad Handfield represents the third generation of his family to welcome guests since 1943. He describes the auberge's cuisine as continental, French Canadian, and healthful. This recipe falls into the cuisine bourgeoise category, leaving aside healthfulness for the moment. Rillettes is a rich spread customarily accompanied by slices of crusty French bread.

1 large goose
4 quarts rich pork stock
4 large onions, cut in pieces
1 teaspoon salt
1 teaspoon white pepper
2 sprigs thyme, or 1/2 teaspoon dried thyme leaves
2 bay leaves
1/2 teaspoon ground cinnamon
3 cups white wine

1. Place the goose and the pork stock in a large pot and add enough water to cover the goose. Add the onions, bring to a boil, reduce the heat, and simmer, covered, for 2 hours. Let cool in the liquid. When cool, remove the goose from the liquid, pass the liquid through a sieve, and return it to the pot. Add the wine and reduce the liquid to about 3 cups over high heat.

2. Remove the meat and grease from the bones and mince the meat.

3. Combine the meat, grease, and reduced cooking liquid in a large bowl. Transfer the mixture to a 9 x 5-inch glass loaf pan and refrigerate overnight or until set. Briefly dip the pan into a larger pan of hot water, then unmold the rillettes onto a plate. Dip a sharp knife in hot water and cut the rillettes into 1/2-inch slices.

Serves 8 to 10.

Camembert Crisp with Gooseberry Chutney and Croûtons

BEEKMAN ARMS, RHINEBECK, NEW YORK

The oldest inn in the country in continuous operation thinks of itself as the place where hospitality began. Over the years it has hosted both the famous and the infamous—among them Benedict Arnold, George Washington, and Franklin Delano Roosevelt, whose Hyde Park home is just a few minutes south of Rhinebeck. The authentic period décor, including the huge stone hearth in the low-ceilinged lobby and the dark-paneled Colonial Tap Room, is balanced by the imaginative American cuisine served in the restaurant.

4 sheets phyllo dough

3 tablespoons unsalted butter, melted

2 5-ounce squares Camembert cheese

Egg wash (1 egg lightly beaten with 2 tablespoons water)

4 large handfuls assorted field greens (mâche, frisée, mezuna,
   baby red oak, radicchio)

4 tablespoons strong vinaigrette

2 teaspoons chopped fresh herbs

Salt and freshly ground pepper to taste

8 tablespoons bottled gooseberry chutney (American Spoon Foods
   brand is available in specialty foods shops)

2 slices whole wheat walnut bread, cut in cubes and baked until crisp
   to make croûtons

1. Lightly brush 1 sheet of phyllo dough with melted butter, cover with a second sheet, and repeat the process with all four sheets. Cut into four even short strips.

2. Cut each piece of Camembert diagonally in half to form a triangle. Lay a Camembert triangle at the end of each of the four pastry strips and begin folding as if folding a flag. Seal the last fold with egg wash.

3. Heat a frying pan on low to medium heat; add the remaining butter and begin crisping the triangles, turning to brown evenly on all sides.

4. Toss the field greens with the vinaigrette, herbs, and salt and pepper. Place the greens on individual plates and lean a warm Camembert triangle against each serving. Garnish with gooseberry chutney and croûtons.

Serves 4.

Appetizer Pizza

JUNIPER HILL INN, WINDSOR, VERMONT

Rob and Susanne Pearl purchased Juniper Hill in 1995 and with the family corgis, Jane and Tucker, are happily welcoming guests to their magnificent hilltop estate overlooking the Connecticut River valley. A twenty-eight room mansion built by Maxwell Evarts in 1902, the house combines twentieth-century grandeur and Colonial simplicity. The grandeur part is obvious from the name of the estate's pond—Lake Runnemeade.

4 small (6-inch) flour tortillas

Olive oil

2 cups red sauce, preferably homemade (prepared spaghetti or pizza sauce may be used)

1 cup shredded cheese (the inn uses Vermont Cheddar and a small amount of Pecorino Romano)

2 ounces chèvre (goat cheese)

6 black olives, pitted and halved

12 to 20 sun-dried tomatoes, soaked in warm water or oil to soften

1. Preheat the oven to 400 degrees F.

2. Brush both sides of the tortillas with olive oil and place on a baking sheet.

3. Top each tortilla with 1/3 to 1/2 cup red sauce. Sprinkle the sauce with the shredded cheese and arrange three to five sun-dried tomatoes on top of each pizza. Crumble 1 tablespoon chèvre over each and arrange 3 black olive halves in the center in a spokelike fashion.

4. Bake until the shredded cheese melts, about 8 minutes, and serve immediately.

Serves 4.

The Wickwood Summer Tart

WICKWOOD INN, SAUGATUCK, MICHIGAN

After many years in Manhattan as co-owner of the renowned Silver Palate gourmet food shop, Julee Rosso Miller has returned to her native Michigan, where she and her husband, Bill Miller, own and operate a country inn in the European tradition. The Millers have visited many of the world's best hotels and have applied all the finest features to their own small inn—French and English antiques, oriental rugs, overstuffed chairs, fresh flowers, candlelight, fine music, original artwork, and the aroma of baking in the air.

1/2 cup Red Pepper Pesto (see recipe below)
2 9 x 9-inch sheets frozen puff pastry, thawed
1 1/2 cups shredded mozzarella cheese
10 ripe Roma tomatoes, cut in 1/4-inch slices
1 1/2 cups shredded Parmesan cheese
1/4 cup minced fresh basil
1 cup Parmesan shards

1. Preheat the oven to 375 degrees F.

2. Roll out the two sheets of puff pastry to fit a 16 1/2 x 12 x 1-inch baking sheet. Cut and piece as necessary, using cold water to seal the seams. Make certain that the sides of the crust are even with or higher than the sides of the baking sheet.

3. Evenly spread the Red Pepper Pesto over the pastry. Sprinkle evenly with the mozzarella, then place the tomato slices in rows on top of the cheese. Sprinkle with the shredded Parmesan and then the basil.

4. Top with the Parmesan shards and bake for 45 minutes, until the cheese and the edges of the crust are golden. Cut in squares and serve immediately.

Serves 24.

Note: Parmesan shards are made by shaving curls from a block of Parmesan cheese, using a vegetable peeler.

Red Pepper Pesto

3 medium red bell peppers
1 tablespoon fresh lemon juice
1/8 teaspoon cayenne pepper
1 plump clove garlic
1/2 tablespoon olive oil
1 1/2 tablespoons sugar, or to taste

1. Preheat the broiler.

2. Slice the peppers in half horizontally and remove the stem, seeds, and membrane. Cut 1/4-inch vertical slits 1 inch apart around the bottom of each pepper half and flatten with your hand.

3. Broil the halves, skin side up, about 4 inches from the heat source until completely blackened. Place the peppers in a large brown paper or plastic bag and close tightly. Allow to steam for 15 to 20 minutes, then remove from bag and peel off the skin.

4. In a blender or food processor, purée the peppers. Add the lemon juice, cayenne, and garlic and process until well blended. Add 1 tablespoon of the sugar and taste before adding the remaining sugar (some peppers are sweeter than others).

5. Use the pesto immediately or refrigerate for up to one week.

Makes about 1 cup.

Spinach and Chèvre Tarts

THE SQUIRE TARBOX INN, WISCASSET, MAINE

Situated in a peaceful wooded area of Westport Island in an eighteenth century house, the Squire Tarbox is only 45 minutes northeast of L.L. Bean but light years away. Karen and Bill Mitman have created a beautiful, restful retreat but wisely realize that "a good country inn must be 'tasted.'" The menu for their five-course dinner changes nightly, and this appetizer is always popular.

1 cup chopped onions
2 tablespoons butter
1 egg, lightly beaten
2 ounces chèvre (goat cheese), at room temperature
Salt and freshly ground pepper to taste
1/2 teaspoon ground nutmeg
1 10-ounce package frozen chopped spinach, thawed, drained, and
   excess water squeezed out
1 tablespoon Caerphilly cheese
Frozen puff pastry
Egg wash made by beating 1 egg with 2 tablespoons water

1. In a sauté pan cook the onions in the butter until they turn light brown. Remove from the heat.

2. Combine half of the beaten egg (discard the rest) with the chèvre and add to the onions. Cook, stirring, for about 3 minutes over low heat. Add the salt and pepper and nutmeg.

3. Add the spinach and cook, stirring, for 5 minutes. Set aside to cool.

4. Stir in the Caerphilly. Preheat the oven to 350 degrees F.

5. Cut the puff pastry into four or six 5-inch squares. Cut a 1/2-inch strip from all four sides and lay the strips along the edges of each square, to form a raised edge. Brush with the egg wash. Place the puff pastry squares on a baking sheet and bake for 10 minutes.

6. Punch in the centers of the baked pastries, to form a well for the filling. Stuff with the spinach mixture and heat in the oven at 300 degrees F for 10 minutes.

Serves 4 to 6.

Soups

Soups

Tomato Soup

Tortilla Soup

Fresh Fennel and Garlic Soup

Old Yankee Fiddlehead Fern Soup

Cream of Wild Mushroom Soup

Mushroom Leek Soup

Red Pepper Bisque

Pear Leek Soup

Lentil Soup

Pumpkin Soup

Santa Fe Black Bean Soup

Corn Chowder with Peconic Bay Scallops

Jamaican Sweet Potato Soup

Oyster and Watercress Velouté Soup

Seafood Asparagus Chowder

Whitefish Chowder

Oyster Stew with Winter Vegetables

Crab and Shrimp Soup

Crème St. Jacques

Cucumber Bisque

Chilled Soup of Northern White Beans and Leeks with Crème Fraîche and Caviar

Gazpacho

Chilled Zucchini Bisque with Chesapeake Crab and Roasted Pepper

Chilled Leek, Tomato, and Smoked Shrimp Soup

Cold Plum Soup

Orchard Inn Peach Soup

Cold Apple and Orange Soup

Tomato Soup

BEAVER POND FARM INN, WARREN, VERMONT

Betty Hansen's culinary talent is a major attraction at Beaver Pond Farm. A caterer in the days when she and her banker husband, Bob, lived in New Jersey, she serves as guest instructor at several cooking schools. Her versatile tomato soup may be served hot or cold, and the cream may be left out in either version. If you choose to serve the soup hot without cream, top it with croûtons; if cold, top with chopped chives.

1/2 cup (1 stick) butter

1 tablespoon olive oil

2 cups thinly sliced onions

1/2 teaspoon dried basil leaves

1/2 teaspoon dried thyme

Salt and freshly ground pepper to taste

1 28-ounce can plum tomatoes, or 2 1/2 pounds fresh tomatoes, chopped

3 tablespoons tomato paste

1/4 cup all-purpose flour

4 cups chicken stock

1 cup heavy cream

4 tablespoons butter

1 teaspoon sugar

1. Melt the 1/2 cup butter in a soup pot. Add the olive oil and stir to mix. Add the onions, basil, thyme, salt, and pepper. Cook, stirring, over low heat, until the onions are wilted but not brown. Add the tomatoes and tomato paste. Stir to combine, and simmer for 10 minutes.

2. Mix the flour with 1/2 cup of the chicken stock. Add to the soup pot and whisk to combine. Stir in the remaining chicken broth and simmer for 30 minutes. Stir occasionally to prevent scorching.

3. Run the mixture through a food mill or process in batches in a food processor.

4. To serve hot, add the cream, 4 tablespoons of butter and the sugar and reheat over low heat, stirring occasionally to prevent scorching.

Serves 8.

Tortilla Soup

THE GALISTEO INN, GALISTEO, NEW MEXICO

Galisteo was founded as a Spanish colonial outpost in 1614, and its residents now include writers, artists, entrepreneurs, and healers. A strong sense of its Native American heritage and Spanish traditions remains and is nowhere more evident than at the Galisteo Inn, a 240-year-old hacienda. The cuisine of chefs Steve and Kirstin Jarrett, however, is strictly up to the minute, using regional ingredients and traditions to create an imaginative, sophisticated menu. Their version of the southwestern staple, tortilla soup, is a hearty, flavorful dish that can be made spicy or mild.

1/2 red onion

1/2 yellow onion

1 ancho chili

1 small green bell pepper

1 small red bell pepper

1 jalapeño pepper

4 cloves garlic

3 tomatoes

12 yellow corn tortillas

1/4 cup canola oil

2 cups tomato juice

3 cups water

1/2 bunch cilantro, chopped

1/8 teaspoon cayenne pepper

1 1/2 teaspoons ground cumin

1/2 teaspoon ground coriander

Juice of 1 lime

Salt and freshly ground pepper to taste

Fried tortilla strips, chopped cilantro, grated white Cheddar cheese,
   diced avocado, for garnish

1. Roughly chop the onions, peppers, garlic, tomatoes, and tortillas.

2. Heat the oil in a pot with a heavy bottom, add the vegetables and tortillas, and sauté over low heat until softened.

3. Add the tomato juice, water, and cilantro and simmer for 20 minutes. Remove from the heat and purée in a blender in small batches, returning the mixture to another pot.

4. Stir in the cayenne, cumin, coriander, lime juice, and salt and pepper and heat to meld seasonings.

5. Serve with crisply fried tortilla strips, cilantro, grated cheese, and avocado.

Serves 8.

Fresh Fennel and Garlic Soup

SWIFT HOUSE INN, MIDDLEBURY, VERMONT

The three buildings comprising Swift House Inn—the 1814 main house, an 1886 carriage house, and the Victorian gatehouse built at the turn of the century—are linked by spacious lawns and a common concern for attractive period décor and warm hospitality. And the next best thing to living in a college town is to enjoy a stay in one of the finest in New England.

2 tablespoons olive or vegetable oil
4 cloves garlic, minced
1 small onion, diced
1 fennel bulb, trimmed and diced
1 baking potato, peeled and diced
4 cups chicken stock
1 teaspoon dried thyme
1 bay leaf
1 pint heavy cream
Salt and white pepper to taste
Dash of Tabasco sauce

1. In a small frying pan heat the oil and sauté the garlic over low heat until it is soft but not brown.

2. Place the onion, fennel, potato, and chicken stock in a soup pot. Add the herbs and the garlic (oil strained off) and cook over medium heat until the vegetables are very soft. Run the mixture through a food mill or process in batches in a food processor until smooth.

3. Return the mixture to a saucepan, add the cream, salt, pepper, and Tabasco, and reheat over low heat.

Serves 4 to 6.

Old Yankee Fiddlehead Fern Soup

ROWELL'S INN, SIMONSVILLE (CHESTER), VERMONT

Antiques and a choice collection of Americana abound at this former stagecoach stop between Chester and Londonderry, Vermont. Beth and Lee Davis refer to their treasures as "Rowell's Inn Relics—one man's junk is another man's treasure." The Tavern Room houses an old soda fountain, a vintage Coke machine, and a mechanical palm reader; the lobby is made from the old Simonsville post office. The menu in the tin-ceilinged dining room includes New England specialties, and this soup is a favorite once spring finally comes.

1/2 cup (1 stick) butter

2 leeks, rinsed, patted dry, and sliced, including about 1/3 of the tender green leaves

1 large onion, chopped

1 clove garlic, minced

2 medium potatoes, peeled and diced

4 dozen fiddleheads, rinsed and patted dry

6 cups chicken broth

Salt and freshly ground pepper to taste

1/2 cup extra heavy cream (use heavy cream if unavailable)

1. In a large saucepan melt the butter. Add the leeks, onion, garlic, potatoes, and fiddleheads and sauté for 5 minutes.

2. Add the broth and bring to a boil, skimming the surface if necessary. Season with salt and pepper. Cover and simmer for about 1 hour, or until the vegetables are very tender.

3. Purée the mixture in batches in a blender and return to the saucepan. Stir in the cream and gently reheat.

Serves 8 to 10.

Cream of Wild Mushroom Soup

GREENVILLE ARMS 1889 INN, GREENVILLE, NEW YORK

Many inns make use of their own herb gardens, and the Greenville Arms is no exception. Innkeeper Eliot Dalton advises that the fresh tarragon called for in this recipe makes a real difference both in flavor and presentation. He also recommends adding a few fresh morels to the soup if they are available and warns against using real wild mushrooms—only expert mycologists should be so daring.

10 ounces white mushrooms, thinly sliced

10 ounces shiitake and/or crimini mushrooms, thinly sliced

1 onion, finely diced

3/4 cup (1 1/2 sticks) butter

2/3 cup all-purpose flour

Pinch of minced fresh tarragon

6 cups chicken broth, preferably homemade

3 cups light cream

Salt and white pepper to taste

8 sprigs fresh tarragon, for garnish

1. Sauté the mushrooms and onion in the butter in a large sauté pan over medium heat (the butter should sizzle but not burn). When the onion is wilted but not brown, stir in the flour and cook, stirring, until the mixture is bubbly and golden.

2. Stir in the pinch of tarragon and the chicken broth and cook over low heat to thicken, about 20 minutes.

3. Before serving, stir in the cream and season with salt and pepper. Gently reheat over low heat. Ladle into bowls and float a tarragon sprig on top of each.

Serves 8.

Mushroom Leek Soup

JUNIPER HILL INN, WINDSOR, VERMONT

At Juniper Hill, dinners are optional but highly desirable. A four-course meal is served by candlelight in the handsome dining room where the feeling of comfort, simple elegance, and romance evident through the inn is at its best.

3 tablespoons butter
1 pound button mushrooms, sliced
2 to 3 leeks (depending on size), cleaned and sliced
1/4 cup flour
3 tablespoons melted butter
1 cup chicken broth
3 cups milk
1/3 cup dry vermouth
Salt and white pepper to taste

1. Place the 3 tablespoons butter, mushrooms, and leeks in a large saucepan with a heavy bottom and sauté until the mushrooms and leeks are soft but not brown.

2. Combine the flour and melted butter to make a very moist paste. Add to the mushrooms and leeks. Cook until pasty, then stir in the chicken broth and the milk and warm through.

3. Add the vermouth and salt and pepper and serve.

Serves 8.

Note: This soup should be fairly thin in consistency, to allow the leek and mushroom slices to float. If the mixture seems too thick, add more milk.

Red Pepper Bisque

HASTINGS HOUSE COUNTRY INN, SALT SPRING ISLAND, BRITISH COLUMBIA

Bearing the distinguished Relais & Chateaux designation, Hastings House has been called a British country estate transplanted into the Canadian wilderness. The Tudor-style Manor House is the centerpiece of the 30-acre property, which offers casually elegant accommodations in five different buildings. Fresh produce and herbs from the garden, eggs from the henhouse, and fruit from trees and bushes on the estate are used daily in the Hastings House kitchen.

1 onion, roughly chopped
6 red bell peppers, roughly chopped
3 cloves garlic, crushed
1 tablespoon olive oil
1 1/2 quarts chicken or vegetable stock
1 potato, peeled and diced
2/3 cup heavy cream
Salt and freshly ground pepper to taste
Few drops of Tabasco sauce
Dash of Worcestershire sauce

1. Sweat the onion, peppers, and garlic in olive oil over low heat until soft but not colored. Add the stock and potato and simmer for 1 hour.

2. Purée the mixture in batches in a blender or food processor and pass through a sieve.

3. Add the heavy cream and simmer, covered, over low heat for 1/2 hour.

4. Season with salt, pepper, Tabasco, and Worcestershire and serve.

Serves 8.

Note: This soup may be made with any type of bell or sweet peppers, and the addition of hot peppers can really liven it up!

Pear Leek Soup

WINDHAM HILL INN, WEST TOWNSHEND, VERMONT

It is rare to find a hot soup with fruit as an ingredient, and this one combines vegetable and fruit in a most successful way. The chef at Windham Hill garnishes the soup with pears cut in tiny dice and poached in red wine and spices (small amounts of grated orange rind, sugar, cinnamon, cloves, whatever strikes your fancy). The liquid is then reduced to a syrup and swirled into the hot soup.

1/4 cup olive or canola oil
2 large leeks, white part only, cleaned and diced
1 Spanish onion, diced
4 stalks celery, diced
4 ripe Anjou or Bartlett pears, peeled, cored, and diced
1 cup dry white wine
3 cups chicken stock
2 cups half-and-half
Salt and white pepper to taste

1. Combine the oil, leeks, onion, and celery in a pan with a heavy bottom and sauté over low heat until the onions are translucent but not brown, about 10 minutes. Add the pears and continue to cook for 5 minutes.

2. Add the wine and cook until the liquid is reduced by half. Add the chicken stock and again reduce by half.

3. Add the half-and-half and simmer, covered, for approximately 20 minutes.

4. Remove from the stove, let cool, and purée in batches in the blender until very smooth. Pass through a sieve.

5. Reheat over low heat, stirring to avoid scorching, and season with salt and pepper. Serve.

Serves 6 to 8.

Lentil Soup

THE 1661 INN AND HOTEL MANISSES, BLOCK ISLAND, RHODE ISLAND

The Abrams and Draper families own two of the finest hostelries on Block Island. The 1661 Inn, named for the year Block Island was settled, has nine guest rooms furnished with antiques. The larger of the two establishments, Hotel Manisses, is a Victorian structure built during the island's initial heyday as a resort community and now restored to its former glory with period furnishings and appointments throughout.

1/2 pound bacon, cut in pieces

1 onion, diced

5 cloves garlic, minced

2 tablespoons curry powder

6 tablespoons butter

1/4 cup sugar

2 quarts turkey stock

1 pound lentils

2 bay leaves

3 carrots, finely diced

1. Purée the bacon in a food processor and cook over medium heat in a soup pot, until it is brown.

2. Add the onion, garlic, curry powder, butter, and sugar and mix well. Add the turkey stock, lentils, and bay leaves, bring to a boil, reduce the heat, and simmer until the lentils are soft, about 45 minutes.

3. For the last 15 minutes of cooking, add the carrots.

Serves 16 to 20.

Pumpkin Soup

THE OLD TAVERN AT GRAFTON, GRAFTON, VERMONT

The lovely town of Grafton has benefited from the special attention of the Windham Foundation, which restored the Old Tavern in 1965 and has since turned its hand to many houses in the village. Some of the finest examples of eighteenth- and nineteenth-century architecture in Vermont are to be found here. In earlier days, the Tavern accommodated the likes of Daniel Webster, Ulysses S. Grant, Hawthorne, Thoreau, Emerson, and Kipling. Today's guests enjoy individually decorated rooms, furnished with antiques; the intrusions of telephone and television are purposely missing.

2 pounds fresh sweet pumpkin, or 3 cups canned pumpkin purée

3 cups half-and-half or milk, scalded

1 tablespoon butter

2 teaspoons pure maple syrup

1 teaspoon salt

1/8 teaspoon ground nutmeg

1. If you are using fresh pumpkin, peel, seed, and steam it until tender, then mash.

2. Stir the pumpkin into the hot half-and-half, then add the remaining ingredients. Combine well, reheat (do not boil), and serve immediately.

Serves 6 to 8.

Santa Fe Black Bean Soup

GRANT CORNER INN, SANTA FE, NEW MEXICO

This well-known inn offers country ambience just two blocks from Santa Fe's bustling Plaza. The Walter family—Chef Pat, Louise, and their young daughter, Bumpy—provide a warm and charming atmosphere at their renovated colonial manor house. Innovative breakfasts, wine and hors d'oeuvres each evening, chocolates on the pillow, and traditional Thanksgiving and Christmas dinners are part of the Walters' successful approach to innkeeping.

1 tablespoon salt

4 cups water

1/2 pound black beans, soaked overnight in cold water to cover and drained

3 white onions, chopped

4 cloves garlic, minced

1/4 cup chopped fresh cilantro

1/2 cup red bell pepper, minced

1/4 cup olive oil

1 tablespoon distilled white vinegar

1 roasted Anaheim chili, chopped

1 small jalapeño pepper, chopped (optional)

1 6-ounce can tomato paste

2 cups chicken broth

Salt and freshly ground pepper to taste

Fresh cilantro leaves, sour cream, paprika, for garnish

1. Add the salt to the water, bring to a boil, add the beans, and reduce the heat to let the beans simmer until they are soft, about 1 1/2 hours.

2. In a large frying pan, sauté the onion, garlic, cilantro, and bell pepper in the olive oil until the onions are slightly brown. Add the vinegar, chili, jalapeño, tomato paste, and chicken broth. Stir over low heat to blend.

3. Drain the cooked beans, reserving 2 cups of the liquid. Add the reserved liquid and the beans to the onion mixture. Stir, continuing to simmer over low heat, for several minutes.

4. Purée the mixture in small amounts in a blender. Pour the purée back into the pan to reheat, and simmer for 5 minutes over low heat, stirring constantly. Season with salt and pepper.

5. Serve hot, garnished with cilantro leaves, a dollop of sour cream, and a dash of paprika.

Serves 4 to 6.

Corn Chowder with Peconic Bay Scallops

THREE VILLAGE INN, STONY BROOK, NEW YORK

Great Peconic Bay and Little Peconic Bay lie northeast of Stony Brook on Long Island and are home to some of the sweetest scallops on the East Coast. In this dish they are paired with fresh corn for an unbeatable summer chowder.

3 ounces pancetta (Italian bacon) or bacon
4 stalks celery, diced
1 1/2 onions, diced
1/2 red bell pepper, seeded and diced
1 green bell pepper, seeded and diced
1 1/2 pounds potatoes, peeled and diced
Kernels from 8 ears fresh corn
1 1/2 gallons clam broth
1 tablespoon salt
Pinch of cayenne pepper
Pinch of white pepper
3 sprigs thyme
1 1/2 pounds bay scallops
2 cups heavy cream

1. In a large pot, render the fat from the pancetta. Cook the pancetta for 3 minutes and remove from the pot. Add the celery, onion, and peppers and cook until translucent. Add the potatoes, corn, and broth and bring to a boil. Add the seasoning and thyme sprigs. Simmer until the potatoes are tender, 8 to 10 minutes.

2. Add the scallops and cream. Heat until steam rises from the surface and serve.

Makes 2 gallons.

Jamaican Sweet Potato Soup

THE AMERICAN GRILL AT CREEKWOOD, MICHIGAN CITY, INDIANA

An hour from Chicago near the southeastern shore of Lake Michigan, Creekwood is a 1930s Tudor country retreat situated on 30 acres of wooded land. Chef Kathy DeFuniak presides over the kitchen in the inn's recently opened restaurant, which serves breakfast daily and dinner on Fridays and Saturdays. Her creativity is evident in this soup, which combines unusual flavors with delicious results.

3 large sweet potatoes, peeled and cubed

1 cup diced onion

6 cups chicken or vegetable stock

2 teaspoons curry powder

1/2 teaspoon ground allspice

1 cup heavy cream

Salt and freshly ground pepper to taste

1/2 cup raisins, for garnish

1/2 cup sliced almonds, toasted, for garnish

1. Place the sweet potatoes, onion, and stock in a large soup pot. Bring to a boil and simmer until the sweet potatoes are very tender. Add the curry powder and allspice and cook for 5 more minutes.

2. Remove from the heat and add the cream. Purée in batches in a blender or food processor until smooth. Add more stock if the soup seems too thick. Season with salt and pepper.

3. Pour into individual bowls and garnish with the raisins and toasted almonds.

Serves 6 to 8.

Oyster and Watercress Velouté Soup

FRIENDS LAKE INN, CHESTERTOWN, NEW YORK

Originally a home-away-from-home boarding house for men working in the local tannery, this 1860 structure soon became an inn for summer people escaping to the Adirondacks from the heat of the crowded cities. Its most recent owners are Sharon and Greg Taylor, who welcome guests at all seasons and for any reason. Like many innkeepers, they can accommodate business meetings and special parties in addition to a general clientèle. Theme parties for bridal rehearsal dinners are a popular innovation—Murder Mystery, Caribbean, wherever the imagination leads.

1 tablespoon plus 4 tablespoons unsalted butter

2 shallots, minced

12 oysters, shucked and liquid reserved

1 cup white wine

Grated rind of 1 lemon

Juice of 1 lemon

1 teaspoon dried thyme leaves

3 cups chicken stock

1/4 cup all-purpose flour

1/2 teaspoon kosher salt

1/8 teaspoon white pepper

1 bunch watercress, stems removed, chopped

1. In a 2-quart heavy pot, melt the 1 tablespoon butter over medium heat. Add the shallots and allow to sweat for 1 minute (do not let them brown).

2. Add the oysters, wine, lemon rind, lemon juice, and thyme. Allow to simmer for 5 minutes. Remove the oysters with a slotted spoon and set aside. Add the chicken stock and continue to simmer.

3. In a frying pan, melt the 4 tablespoons butter over medium heat; stir in the flour and cook for 5 minutes, stirring occasionally.

4. Whisk the flour-butter mixture (roux) into the stock, add the salt and pepper, and simmer for 1/2 hour, stirring occasionally to prevent scorching. Just before serving, add the watercress, the oysters, and the reserved liquid from the oysters.

Serves 4.

Seafood Asparagus Chowder

THE GRISWOLD INN, ESSEX, CONNECTICUT

"The Gris," as it is affectionately known, considers itself a kaleidoscope of nostalgic images, among them a group of charming dining rooms—the Covered Bridge, the Steamboat, the Library, and the Gun Room.

2 pounds asparagus
1 onion, roughly chopped
1 bunch celery, roughly chopped
1/2 pound bacon, chopped
1/2 cup (1 stick) butter
1 cup all-purpose flour
2 quarts chicken stock
8 red potatoes, diced (unpeeled)
5 ounces swordfish
5 ounces scallops
5 ounces salmon
6 ounces lobster meat
1 small can baby corn, drained
1/2 cup light cream
Salt, white pepper, and garlic powder to taste

1. Cut the asparagus stems into 1-inch pieces, reserving the tips. Process the stems in a food processor and set aside. Process the onion and celery and add to the asparagus.

2. Heat a large frying pan and add the bacon. Cook until the fat is rendered. Remove the bacon from the pan, leaving the fat in the pan. Add the butter to the bacon fat and melt over low heat.

3. Add the asparagus, celery, and onion to the frying pan and sauté for 10 minutes, stirring occasionally. Add the flour and stir to incorporate (the mixture should have the consistency of paste). Cook, stirring frequently, over low heat for 20 minutes.

4. Bring the chicken stock to a boil. Add to the asparagus mixture, stir constantly over low heat until thickened, and let simmer for 10 minutes.

5. In separate processes, steam the potatoes, seafood, and asparagus tips, until just tender. Drain well and add to the soup, with the baby corn and light cream. Season with salt, pepper, and garlic, and serve.

Serves 8 to 10.

❦

Whitefish Chowder

THE WHITE GULL INN, FISH CREEK, WISCONSIN

The Door County Fish Boil is a major attraction at the White Gull Inn, summer and winter. Freshly caught whitefish and red-skin potatoes are wrapped in cheesecloth and cooked together in an iron pot over an open fire, with a dramatic overboil at the end. They are served with melted butter and lemon and accompanied by coleslaw, homemade breads, and cherry pie à la mode. Whitefish Chowder makes more sense for the home kitchen—a wonderful dish for cold winter days, in Wisconsin or elsewhere.

1/2 pound bacon, diced

2 cups diced onion

6 large potatoes, peeled and cubed

1 51-ounce can chicken broth

2 pounds whitefish, deboned, cut into 1-inch pieces

1 1/2 quarts half-and-half

1 teaspoon salt

1/2 teaspoon white pepper

1. Sauté the bacon in a heavy-bottomed pan until the fat is rendered. Remove the bacon from the pan and sauté the onion in the fat for 5 minutes. Add the potatoes and the broth and simmer for 5 minutes.

2. Add the whitefish and cook until the potatoes are tender, about 15 minutes. Add the half-and-half and season with the salt and pepper. Simmer (do not boil) to heat through. Add the crumbled bacon just before serving.

Serves 16.

Oyster Stew with Winter Vegetables

THE GRISWOLD INN, ESSEX, CONNECTICUT

Essex is a lovely town on the Connecticut River, not far from coastal New London, which explains why seafood is a specialty at the Griswold Inn. The addition of vegetables to the classic oyster stew makes this a hearty one-dish meal.

Oil to coat bottom of pan
48 oysters, shucked
1/2 teaspoon Tabasco sauce
1/2 teaspoon Worcestershire sauce
1/2 teaspoon sherry pepper sauce
Salt and freshly ground pepper to taste
3 parsnips, thinly sliced
3 carrots, thinly sliced
5 stalks celery, sliced on bias
5 red potatoes (unpeeled), medium diced
1 1/2 quarts heavy cream
4 tablespoons butter

1. In a deep saucepan, heat the oil over high heat. Reduce the heat to medium and add the oysters, Tabasco, Worcestershire, sherry pepper sauce, salt, and pepper. Cook just until the oysters begin to curl around the edges, then remove oysters from the pan and set aside.

2. Add the vegetables to the remaining juices in the pan. Sauté over high heat for 2 minutes, stirring frequently. Reduce the heat and add the heavy cream. Simmer over low heat until the cream begins to reduce.

3. Once the mixture has thickened, add the oysters and simmer for an additional minute. Remove from the heat and whisk in the butter. Serve immediately.

Serves 6 to 8.

Crab and Shrimp Soup

ROBERT MORRIS INN, OXFORD, MARYLAND

Oxford, on Maryland's Eastern Shore, was a bustling international shipping center in colonial days, when Robert Morris moved there to represent the interests of a British tobacco importing company. The mansion he lived in, built before 1710 by ships' carpenters, has been expanded many times over the years but still retains much of the original paneling and several fireplaces. Ken and Wendy Gibson, who have owned the inn since 1975, have preserved the historic charm of the house. Simple comfort, quiet hospitality, and good food (especially seafood from the bay) are the inn's hallmarks.

1 cup water

1/2 cup chopped onion

1/2 teaspoon seafood seasoning

1/2 teaspoon crushed dried thyme leaves

1/2 teaspoon crushed dried marjoram leaves

Dash of white pepper

1 pound shrimp, peeled, deveined, and cut up

2 10 3/4-ounce cans condensed cream of chicken soup

1 soup can milk

1/4 pound fresh or frozen Maryland crabmeat, picked over and
  shells removed

2 tablespoons dry white wine

1. In a 2-quart saucepan, combine the water, onion, and seasonings. Heat to boiling, reduce the heat to low, cover, and simmer for 10 minutes.

2. Add the shrimp and simmer for 10 minutes more. Stir in the cream of chicken soup, milk, crabmeat, and wine. Heat over low heat, stirring, and ladle into soup bowls.

Serves 4.

Crème St. Jacques

THE INN ON THE COMMON, CRAFTSBURY COMMON, VERMONT

Breakfast and dinner at the Inn on the Common are enjoyed at long tables in the elegant dining room, providing a chance to meet fellow guests; an honor-system cocktail hour in the library precedes dinner. According to the **Boston Globe**, *"The meals prepared by chef Yves Morrissette rival Boston's best restaurants."*

1 1/2 quarts water

1 pound potatoes, peeled and quartered

1 cup chopped onion

1 tablespoon dried thyme leaves

Salt and white pepper to taste

1 cup sea scallops

2 egg yolks

1/2 cup heavy cream

Freshly grated Parmesan cheese, for garnish

1. Place the water, potatoes, onion, thyme, salt, and pepper in a large saucepan, bring to a boil, and simmer until the potatoes are tender, 20 to 30 minutes. Add the scallops and simmer for 5 minutes.

2. Purée the mixture in batches in a blender or food processor until smooth.

3. Whisk together the egg yolks and cream and add to the soup, whisking as you pour. Adjust the seasoning and reheat (do not boil). Ladle into soup bowls and garnish with Parmesan cheese. Serve with croûtons or a salad.

Serves 8.

Note: This soup is best served right after it is made.

Cucumber Bisque

STAFFORDS-IN-THE-FIELD, CHOCORUA,
NEW HAMPSHIRE

As its name suggests, Staffords-in-the-Field occupies a knoll in the midst of rolling hay fields, with Mount Chocorua and the Sandwich and Presidential ranges rising in the distance. The Stafford family rescued the property in 1965 after it had lain idle for several years between innkeepers. A Federal Period house with the addition of a broad veranda, an old apple orchard, and a working sugarhouse combine to give this country place a special atmosphere.

3 tablespoons butter
2 large cucumbers, peeled, seeded, and sliced
1 large yellow onion, sliced
1 large dill pickle, sliced
3 tablespoons all-purpose flour
3 cups chicken stock
Salt to taste
1/2 cup light cream
Minced fresh dill, for garnish

1. Melt the butter in a 3-quart saucepan. Add the cucumber, onion, and dill pickle and sauté until the vegetables are translucent (do not let them brown). Sprinkle the flour over the vegetables and continue cooking for 5 minutes.

2. Add the chicken stock to the vegetables, bring to a boil, and cook for 20 minutes.

3. Purée the mixture in batches in a blender or food processor. Chill.

4. Taste the chilled soup for salt, stir in the cream, and serve in chilled bowls. Garnish with the fresh dill.

   Serves 8 to 12.

Note: This soup does not freeze well.

Chilled Soup of Northern White Beans and Leeks with Crème Fraîche and Caviar

L'ÉTOILE AT THE CHARLOTTE INN, EDGARTOWN, MASSACHUSETTS

It is becoming increasingly common for restaurateurs to join forces with innkeepers to offer the best of both professions under a common roof. This is the case at the Charlotte Inn, where l'étoile, a contemporary French restaurant, operates under the direction of chef Michael Brisson and his partner, Joan Parzanese. Chef Brisson has created this pleasant variation of the classic Vichyssoise for the hot summer months when Edgartown is at its busiest.

1/4 cup olive oil

4 shallots, minced (about 1/2 cup)

1 cup white wine

3 cups white beans, soaked in 8 cups cool water overnight, then drained

4 to 6 cups chicken stock

2 cups chopped cleaned leeks

Salt and freshly ground pepper to taste

1 cup heavy cream

1/2 cup crème fraîche, for garnish

1 ounce black American caviar, for garnish

Whole or chopped chives, for garnish

1. Heat the olive oil in a heavy-bottomed pot and sweat the shallots until they are translucent. Add the wine and reduce over high heat for 3 minutes. Add the beans and generously cover them with the chicken stock. Cover the pot and simmer over medium heat until the beans are tender, about 50 minutes.

2. Stir in the leeks, cover, and cook until tender, about 10 minutes. Remove from the heat and let cool.

3. Purée the soup in batches in a blender or food processor until smooth (reserve some liquid to adjust the texture later if necessary). Season with salt and pepper and stir in the cream.

4. Check the seasoning and texture; add more stock if the soup is too thick, more cream if you prefer a richer soup. Refrigerate, stirring every half hour until cool.

5. Serve in chilled red wine glasses with three small dollops of crème fraîche topped with caviar and chives.

Serve 8.

Gazpacho

SHERWOOD INN, SKANEATELES, NEW YORK

At Sherwood Inn, this proverbial favorite is used as an appetizer, as a dressing for seafood salad, or as a luncheon entrée, accompanied with warm bread. The consistency desired depends on how the gazpacho is to be served. For soup, beware of overblending the mixture.

5 ripe tomatoes, peeled, seeded, and roughly chopped
1 green bell pepper, seeded and roughly chopped
3 scallions, roughly chopped
1 large cucumber, peeled, seeded, and roughly chopped
1 clove garlic
1 teaspoon freshly grated pepper
1/2 cup olive oil
1 tablespoon wine vinegar
Salt, fresh basil leaves, and Tabasco sauce to taste

1. Place all the ingredients in the bowl of a food processor and blend until the desired consistency is achieved.

2. Pour into chilled bowls and serve.

Serves 4.

Chilled Zucchini Bisque with Chesapeake Crab and Roasted Pepper

TURNING POINT INN, FREDERICK, MARYLAND

Less than an hour from Washington, D.C., Baltimore, Gettysburg, and Virginia horse country, close to excellent antiquing and many significant historical sites, Turning Point Inn is a gracious and comfortable place to come home to after a day of exploring. Under the direction of Executive Chef Paul Stalnaker, breakfast is served daily, with lunch and dinner available certain days of the week. Chef Stalnaker advises that this soup is also good served hot, heated over low heat just to the boiling point.

4 tablespoons unsalted butter

1 leek, cleaned, trimmed, and sliced

1/2 cup diced onion

1 teaspoon minced garlic

4 pounds zucchini, seeded and diced

1 pound potatoes, peeled and diced

2 tablespoons fresh tarragon leaves

2 quarts chicken stock

2 cups heavy cream

Salt and white pepper to taste

1 red bell pepper, roasted, skinned, seeded, and diced (see note page 13)

1 pound backfin or lump crabmeat, well picked over

Fresh tarragon sprigs, for garnish

1. Heat the butter in a large sauté pan and sauté the leek, onion, and garlic until the vegetables are translucent. Add the zucchini and potatoes and sauté for 15 minutes.

2. Add the tarragon leaves and chicken stock and simmer for 30 to 45 minutes over medium heat.

3. Cool the mixture, then purée in batches in a blender or food processor until smooth. Add the cream, salt, and pepper. Chill overnight.

4. Place a spoonful of roasted red pepper in the bottom of each of 16 chilled bowls; add 1 ounce of crabmeat to each bowl and ladle the soup over the mixture. Garnish with fresh tarragon sprigs.

Serves 16.

Chilled Leek, Tomato, and Smoked Shrimp Soup

BARROWS HOUSE, DORSET, VERMONT

Barrows House takes its name from Experience and Theresa Barrows, who bought the property in 1900 and established it as an inn. A total of eight buildings dot the grounds, connected by spacious lawns and expansive perennial gardens. Each cottage or room has its own story and is furnished in its own style, with antiques, old family pieces, and, thankfully, modern bedding. Breakfast and dinner are served in the early nineteenth-century main house every day of the year.

2 tablespoons clarified butter (see note page 94)
1 leek, cleaned and sliced thin
1/2 Spanish onion, sliced thin
3 large fresh tomatoes, peeled, seeded, and diced
1 large bay leaf
2 cups fish stock or chicken broth
3/4 cup heavy cream
1 cup chopped smoked Maine shrimp
Salt and freshly ground pepper to taste

1. In a saucepan, place the clarified butter, leek, onion, tomatoes, and bay leaf. Cover and cook over medium heat until the tomato releases its juices, about 5 minutes.

2. Uncover and cook for 10 minutes, until the leek and onion are translucent. Raise the heat and bring to a boil. Remove from the heat and discard the bay leaf.

3. Purée the mixture in a blender or food processor and strain through a medium-holed sieve into a large bowl. Stir in the stock, cream, shrimp, salt, and pepper.

4. Chill the soup and serve in chilled bowls.

Serves 4 to 6.

Cold Plum Soup

THREE VILLAGE INN, STONY BROOK, NEW YORK

Stony Brook, Old Field, and Setauket are the three villages on Long Island's North Shore that have come to be known simply as Stony Brook. At one time a busy port, the town was home to 53 sea captains, and many of their nineteenth-century houses remain. The earliest part of the main building at Three Village Inn was built in 1751, and since then the property has been a Presbyterian retreat, a women's exchange, and, beginning in 1939, an inn and fine restaurant.

1 1-pound 13-ounce tin purple plums
1 1/2 cups water
1/2 cup sugar
1 stick cinnamon
1/4 teaspoon white pepper
Pinch of salt
1/2 cup dry red wine
1 tablespoon cornstarch
1 cup heavy cream
2 tablespoons fresh lemon juice
1 teaspoon grated lemon rind
1 cup sour cream
3 tablespoons brandy
Sour cream, for garnish
Ground cinnamon, for garnish

1. Drain the plums, reserving the syrup, and pit and chop the plums. In a saucepan, combine the plums with the reserved syrup, the water, sugar, cinnamon stick, white pepper, and salt and bring to a boil over moderately high heat. Reduce the heat to medium and cook, stirring occasionally, for 5 minutes.

2. Combine the wine and cornstarch in a small bowl and add this mixture and the cream to the plum mixture. Cook, stirring, until the mixture has thickened.

3. Stir in the lemon juice and rind and remove the pan from the heat.

4. In a small bowl, whisk the sour cream and brandy into 1/2 cup of the soup. Stir the mixture into the rest of the soup and blend until smooth.

5. Let the soup cool and chill it, covered, for at least 4 hours.

6. Ladle the soup into chilled cups and garnish each serving with a dollop of sour cream and a sprinkling of cinnamon.

Serves 6 to 8.

Orchard Inn Peach Soup

THE ORCHARD INN, SALUDA, NORTH CAROLINA

In the foothills of the Blue Ridge Mountains just below the town of Saluda, (terminus to the steepest railway grade east of the Rockies), the Southern Railroad built a getaway for its International Union of Railway Clerks and Engineers in about 1900. This peaceful mountain setting is now home to the Orchard Inn, an inimitable place to enjoy hiking, fishing, and birding in the great outdoors and, indoors, attractive accommodations and French Provincial cuisine with a North Carolina accent.

8 to 12 fresh peaches, peeled, pitted, and sliced (about 5 cups)
1 cup orange juice
1 cup pineapple juice
3 tablespoons sour cream
1/2 teaspoon grated fresh ginger root
Sherry to taste (optional)
Sour cream, fresh mint leaves, or thin slices of peach, for garnish

1. Place the peaches, orange juice, pineapple juice, 3 tablespoons sour cream, and ginger in a blender and blend at high speed for about 15 seconds.

2. Chill the soup and serve in chilled bowls, garnished with your choice of a dollop of sour cream, a mint leaf, or a thin slice of peach.

Serves 6 to 8.

Cold Apple and Orange Soup

EAGLES MERE INN, EAGLES MERE, PENNSYLVANIA

The town of Eagles Mere in the Endless Mountains of northeastern Pennsylvania bills itself as The Last Unspoiled Resort, and the Eagles Mere Inn is part of its history and charm. The inn was built in 1878 as lodging for the craftsmen who erected the cottages and large hotels for wealthy Philadelphians coming to the area for the cool, clean air and crystal clear waters. The hotels and cottages are gone, but the inn remains, updated with 1990s comforts and a commitment to outstanding food.

3 tablespoons fresh lemon juice

3 cups apple juice

1 tablespoon sugar

2 cinnamon sticks

6 apples (Rome, Cortland, or Winesap recommended), peeled, cored, and sliced

3/4 teaspoon pure vanilla extract

2 1/4 cups orange juice

3 cups half-and-half

Thinly sliced unpeeled apple, dipped in lemon juice, for garnish

Tiny parsley leaves, for garnish

1. Combine the lemon juice, apple juice, sugar, and cinnamon sticks in a large pot. Add the apples (to avoid browning, slice them directly into the liquid) and cook, covered, over medium heat until the apples are tender.

2. Remove the pan from the heat, remove the cinnamon sticks, and add the vanilla. Purée in batches in a blender or food processor.

3. Stir in the orange juice and half-and-half and chill for at least 4 hours.

4. Serve in chilled bowls, garnishing each serving with an apple slice and a tiny parsley leaf.

Serves 15.

Vegetables and Salads

Vegetables and Salads

Red Cabbage
Stafford's Tomato Pudding
Fresh Corn Tart
Turnip Soufflé
Jalapeño Corn Mashed Potatoes
Aunt Hattie's Squash Soufflé
Eggplant and Cheese Torte
Potato Leek Pie
Green Onion and Saffron Risotto
Wild Rice and Pecan Pancakes
Grits Casserole
Southern Spoon Bread
Orange Walnut Salad
Will's Sunday Salad with Tofu Dressing
Fiesta Salad
Mediterranean Fusilli Salad
Harbor House Tabouleh

Red Cabbage

LOWELL INN, STILLWATER, MINNESOTA

Founded by descendants of the well-known Massachusetts family, Lowell Inn opened its doors to the public in 1927 and has been owned since 1930 by several generations of Palmers. Its Colonial façade, complete with two-story columns, causes it to be known as The Mount Vernon of the West, and guests wishing a formal meal choose the George Washington Dining Room.

1 medium head red cabbage, outer leaves removed, cored, and sliced
1 onion, sliced
2 large apples, peeled and quartered
1 heaping tablespoon bacon fat
1 teaspoon salt
1/2 cup sugar
1 1/2 cups water
1 cup cider vinegar
1 bay leaf
2 whole allspice
2 whole cloves, heads removed
6 peppercorns
2 teaspoons cornstarch

1. In a large bowl, toss together the cabbage, onion, and apples. Add the remaining ingredients, except the cornstarch.

2. Transfer the mixture to a large sauté pan, cover, and simmer over low heat for 1 1/2 hours, stirring occasionally.

3. Mix about 2 tablespoons of the juice from the pan with the cornstarch, then stir the mixture into the cabbage. Cook briefly to thicken.

Serves 4 to 6.

Stafford's Tomato Pudding

STAFFORD'S BAY VIEW INN, PETOSKEY, MICHIGAN

Visitors return year after year to this country inn overlooking Little Traverse Bay on the northwestern shoreline of Lake Michigan. Part of the reason is the collection of family recipes shared by owner/chef Stafford Smith. He always bakes this pudding a day ahead to allow the flavors to meld as it sits overnight, covered, in the refrigerator. The next day he dots the top with a bit more butter and reheats the casserole for about 20 minutes at 325 degrees F.

1 #10 can stewed tomatoes, drained (see note below)
1/2 cup light brown sugar
4 cups 1-inch dried bread cubes
Basil, thyme, salt, and pepper to taste
Butter

1. Preheat the oven to 350 degrees F. Butter a 4-quart casserole dish.

2. Place the tomatoes in a large bowl and add the brown sugar and bread cubes. Mix well and season to taste with basil, thyme, salt, and pepper.

3. Place the mixture in the casserole dish and dot with butter. Bake for 30 to 45 minutes.

Serves 6.

Note: A #10 can is a commercial size, containing 6 pounds, 9 ounces (3 quarts). Fresh tomatoes may be used, but they first must be peeled, stewed, and drained. The tomatoes reduce a great deal in cooking.

Fresh Corn Tart

THE 1770 HOUSE, EAST HAMPTON, NEW YORK

Renovated by the Perle family after a period of decline, the 1770 House enjoyed its first glory in the late Forties and early Fifties when celebrities from film, theater, and high society were frequent guests. One of the loveliest towns in America was and is a popular summer place, with magnificent beaches, cultural opportunities, and an abundance of sports available. Fresh Corn Tart is a favorite on the summer menu, made with fresh local corn. According to the chef, the vanilla extract is what makes the dish special.

2 tablespoons bread crumbs

1 1/2 cups fresh corn kernels (cut from approximately 3 ears)

1 teaspoon salt

1/4 cup sugar

2 tablespoons melted butter

3 eggs, separated

2 tablespoons all-purpose flour

1/2 cup heavy cream

3/4 cup milk

1 teaspoon pure vanilla extract

Freshly ground pepper

1. Preheat the oven to 400 degrees F. Grease a 1-quart soufflé dish and dust with the bread crumbs.

2. Combine the corn, salt, sugar, and butter; mix well. In a large bowl, beat the egg yolks with the flour until smooth. Stir in the cream, milk, and vanilla extract. Add the corn mixture and combine well.

3. In a separate bowl, beat the egg whites until stiff but not dry; fold into the corn mixture. Pour into the prepared soufflé dish and sprinkle with freshly ground pepper.

4. Bake at 400 degrees F for 20 minutes; reduce the temperature to 375 degrees F and continue baking until a toothpick inserted in the center comes out fairly clean, 35 to 40 minutes.

Serves 6 to 8.

Turnip Soufflé

UNDER MOUNTAIN INN, SALISBURY, CONNECTICUT

*Peter and Marged Higginson have brought a touch of England to northwestern Connecticut. Chef Peter is retired from the British Merchant Navy and his répertoire includes steak and kidney pie, bangers and mash, and an afternoon cream tea; on Saturday mornings a full English breakfast is available. Reminders of England appear throughout the inn—copies of the **Manchester Guardian Weekly** and books about the royal family in the comfortable living room, Gilbert & Soames soaps in the bathrooms, horse brasses in the tavern/pub.*

3 pounds turnips, peeled and cubed

3 pounds white potatoes, peeled and cubed

6 tablespoons (3/4 stick) butter

1 small onion, finely chopped

1/4 cup diced green bell pepper

2 eggs

1 cup mayonnaise

1 cup freshly grated Parmesan cheese

Freshly ground pepper to taste

1/4 cup (or more) dry bread crumbs

2 tablespoons melted butter

Paprika

1. Cook the turnips and potatoes in separate pans in water to cover until tender, about 30 minutes. Drain well and transfer to a large bowl. Mash with 4 tablespoons of the butter and let the mixture cool.

2. In a small skillet, heat the remaining 2 tablespoons of butter and sauté the onion and green pepper. Set aside.

3. Preheat the oven to 350 degrees F. Butter a 9-inch square pan.

4. In a small bowl, whip the eggs with the mayonnaise; stir in the cheese and freshly ground pepper.

5. Add the onion, green pepper, and egg mixture to the cooled turnip and potato mixture. Mix well.

6. Transfer the mixture to the prepared pan. Combine the bread crumbs and melted butter and distribute evenly over the top of the casserole; sprinkle with paprika. Bake for 30 minutes or until the top is golden brown at the edges.

Serves 8.

Jalapeño Corn Mashed Potatoes

GRANT CORNER INN, SANTA FE, NEW MEXICO

Built in the early 1900s as a home for a wealthy New Mexican ranching family, Grant Corner Inn has eleven guest rooms furnished with brass and four-poster beds, armoires, antique quilts, and artwork and treasures from around the world. A southwestern style condominium called The Hacienda, five blocks away, is also part of the inn.

4 3-ounce packages cream cheese, cut in cubes
1/4 cup milk
5 tablespoons butter
5 cups mashed potatoes
4 jalapeño peppers, seeded and minced
11/2 cups cooked corn, drained
2 teaspoons salt
2 teaspoons, or less, white pepper

1. Preheat the oven to 350 degrees F. Butter a 13 x 9-inch glass baking dish.

2. Place the cream cheese, milk, and butter in a saucepan and cook, stirring, over low heat until the cheese has melted.

3. Place the mashed potatoes in a large bowl and stir in the cheese mixture. Add the jalapeños, corn, salt, and pepper. Mix well and spoon into the prepared baking dish. Bake for about 30 minutes.

Serves 6.

Aunt Hattie's Squash Soufflé

HEMLOCK INN, BRYSON CITY, NORTH CAROLINA

At Hemlock Inn, dinner is served family style at bountifully laden Lazy Susan tables. Country ham, fried chicken, and other regional foods are featured, and Squash Soufflé is often an accompaniment. Lorene Haynie, who built the inn, was given this recipe by her Aunt Hattie, and it has been a favorite of guests for over forty years. Though the vintage recipe calls for ground onion and pepper, the technique can be replicated in today's food processor or by mincing with a sharp knife.

1/2 cup dry milk

1 cup bread crumbs

2 cups squash broth

1 quart cooked and drained summer squash (reserve broth)

2 tablespoons ground onion

1 tablespoon ground green bell pepper

2 eggs, well beaten

2 tablespoons sugar

1 teaspoon salt

2 tablespoons melted margarine

1/2 teaspoon seasoned salt

1. Preheat the oven to 300 degrees F. Butter a 2-quart casserole.

2. Combine the milk, crumbs, and squash broth and let soak for 15 minutes.

3. Place the squash in a large bowl and stir in the milk mixture. Add the onion, green pepper, beaten eggs, sugar, salt, margarine, and seasoned salt and mix well.

4. Transfer the mixture to the prepared casserole and bake for 35 minutes.

Serves 10.

Eggplant and Cheese Torte

WALDEN INN, GREENCASTLE, INDIANA

The prevailing philosophy at Walden Inn harks back to a simpler time, as chronicled in Henry David Thoreau's famous account of his year on Walden Pond. Quotations from the book are used to describe all aspects of what a guest at the inn might experience. As for dinner in the Different Drummer restaurant, "...the gods have really intended that men should feed divinely..." This particular dish is served with grilled chicken or fish and may also be used as an appetizer.

2 large eggplants
3 whole tomatoes, minced
1/2 cup chopped fresh basil leaves
1/3 cup tomato juice
1 cup grated mozzarella cheese
1/2 cup grated Gruyère cheese
2 tablespoons freshly grated Parmesan cheese

1. Preheat the oven to 350 degrees F. Lightly grease a 9-inch springform pan.

2. Slice the eggplants as thinly as possible, crosswise.

3. Combine the tomato, basil, and tomato juice. Combine the three cheeses.

4. Cover the bottom of the prepared pan with one layer of overlapping slices of eggplant. Brush with some tomato sauce and sprinkle with cheese.

5. Repeat the layering of eggplant, tomato sauce, and cheese until all have been used, making sure there is a cheese layer on top.

6. Bake for 15 minutes, or until the cheeses have melted. Remove the sides of the pan and cut and serve the torte in wedges.

Serves 6.

Potato Leek Pie

THE CHECKERBERRY INN, GOSHEN, INDIANA

Here is an inn that combines the comforts of new construction with the country charm of the surrounding Amish farmland. Rustic side chairs and antique quilts coexist with comfortable sofas banked with pillows and well-placed reading lights. The 100-acre property includes a pastoral walking lane as well as the more sophisticated amenities of swimming pool, tennis court, and croquet lawn.

4 large baking potatoes (russets)

3 eggs

1 cup shredded cheese, preferably Swiss

1 cup milk

1/2 cup half-and-half

2 teaspoons salt

1 teaspoon freshly ground pepper

1/4 teaspoon ground nutmeg

1/2 cup thinly sliced leek, white part only

Butter

1/4 cup freshly grated Parmesan cheese

1. Preheat the oven to 325 degrees F. Spray a 6 x 12-inch casserole with vegetable spray, coating the bottom and sides.

2. Peel and thinly slice the potatoes, using a food processor or the side of a box grater. Submerge in water immediately.

3. Beat the eggs, Swiss cheese, milk, and half-and-half together. Add 1 teaspoon of the salt and the pepper and nutmeg.

4. Sauté the leeks in a small amount of butter until they are soft, 3 to 5 minutes.

5. Drain the potatoes, combine with the leeks, and transfer to the prepared casserole. Sprinkle in the remaining salt and mix well. Cover with the egg mixture and flatten the potatoes with a spoon to make the top smooth.

6. Sprinkle the Parmesan cheese on top and bake for 25 to 35 minutes or until brown on top. Cool and slice into squares. Serve at room temperature.

Serves 6 to 8.

Green Onion and Saffron Risotto

FRIENDS LAKE INN, CHESTERTOWN, NEW YORK

The dining room at Friends Lake Inn combines the ambience of the nineteenth century with the sophisticated cuisine of the late twentieth century. Risotto needs constant attention during cooking but the result is worth the time. This particular version is customarily served with the inn's Roast Baby Quail with Apricot Sausage (see page 112).

2 tablespoons butter

2 teaspoons olive oil

2 teaspoons saffron threads

1 small onion, minced

1 cup Arborio rice (Italian rice, available at specialty foods shops)

2 1/2 cups hot chicken stock

2 teaspoons kosher salt

1/2 teaspoon white pepper

1/4 cup heavy cream

1/2 cup minced green onions (scallions)

1. Heat the butter, olive oil, and saffron in a large saucepan. Add the onion and sauté over medium heat until the onion is soft but not brown, about 5 minutes.

2. Add the rice and cook for 3 minutes, stirring and turning until each grain is coated with oil. Blend in 1/2 cup stock and the salt and pepper.

3. Gradually add more stock, 1/2 cup at a time, as each amount becomes absorbed by the rice. Stir frequently, allowing 20 to 30 minutes' total cooking time.

4. When all the stock has been absorbed, stir in the cream and green onion. The rice should be creamy but still firm. Serve immediately.

Serves 4.

Wild Rice and Pecan Pancakes

WALDEN INN, GREENCASTLE, INDIANA

Greencastle lies among the rolling hills of western Indiana and is home to DePauw University, whose parents and guests enjoy the comforts of Walden Inn and appreciate the excellent food available there. Melons, persimmons, and produce from local farms are relied upon, as well as imported ingredients and seafood from other parts of the country and the world.

3 cups water
2/3 cup wild rice
1 1/2 teaspoons salt
1/2 cup all-purpose flour
1/2 teaspoon baking powder
1/2 teaspoon baking soda
1 egg, beaten
1/2 cup milk
1/4 cup chopped and toasted pecans
2 tablespoons minced shallots
Olive oil

1. Combine the water, rice, and salt in a saucepan. Bring to a boil over medium heat, reduce the heat, and simmer, covered, until the rice is tender, about 40 minutes. Drain and cool to room temperature.

2. Combine the flour, baking powder, and baking soda in a small bowl. In a large bowl, mix together the egg and milk. Stir in the flour mixture.

3. Add the rice, pecans, and shallots to the flour mixture and combine well.

4. Preheat a frying pan, lightly coated with olive oil. By tablespoonfuls, drop in the pancake mixture and cook on both sides until golden brown.

Makes 12 pancakes.

Note: The rice may be cooked the day before and refrigerated.

Grits Casserole

CLEWISTON INN, CLEWISTON, FLORIDA

Built in 1938 on the shore of Lake Okeechobee as an executive retreat for the U.S. Sugar Corporation, the Clewiston Inn has the look and feel of the Old South. The menu, too, has a southern feel, and the Friday noon buffet features Lake Okeechobee "Sharpies" Catfish and Grits Casserole.

4 cups water

1 cup white grits

2 teaspoons salt

3/4 cup (1 1/2 sticks) butter, cut in pieces

1 cup grated sharp Cheddar cheese

1 cup milk or half-and-half

4 eggs, beaten

4 cloves garlic, put through garlic press

1 1/2 cups cornflake crumbs

1. Bring the water to a boil in a large saucepan and gradually stir in the grits and salt. Cook over low heat, stirring frequently, until very thick, about 30 minutes.

2. Preheat the oven to 350 degrees F. Butter a baking dish.

3. Immediately after the grits have reached the proper thickness, add the butter and cheese and stir until melted. Blend in the milk, eggs, and garlic.

4. Pour the mixture into the prepared baking dish and top with the cornflake crumbs. Bake until set, with the crumbs lightly browned, about 45 minutes.

Serves 8.

Southern Spoon Bread

BOONE TAVERN HOTEL, BEREA, KENTUCKY

Boone Tavern is part of a unique educational experience whereby students at Berea College work in various college enterprises, including the hotel, in lieu of paying tuition. The college has been serving young people from the Appalachian region since 1855 and is known to travelers for its fine craft industries, art and music programs, and the superb hospitality offered at Boone Tavern. Spoon Bread is a favorite regional specialty.

3 cups milk
1 1/4 cups cornmeal
3 eggs, well beaten
1 teaspoon salt
1 3/4 teaspoons baking powder
2 tablespoons butter, melted

1. Bring the milk to a boil in a large saucepan. Stir in the cornmeal and cook until very thick, stirring constantly to prevent scorching. Remove from the heat and allow to cool. The mixture will be very stiff.

2. Preheat the oven to 375 degrees F. Butter two 1-quart casseroles.

3. Add the egg, salt, baking powder, and melted butter to the grits. Beat with an electric mixer for 15 minutes.

4. Pour into the prepared casseroles and bake for 30 minutes. Serve immediately.

Serves 8 to 10.

Orange Walnut Salad

EAGLES MERE INN, EAGLES MERE, PENNSYLVANIA

Eagles Mere welcomes guests at all seasons, but springtime is exceptionally beautiful. Banks of mountain laurel, rhododendron, and azaleas join the customary spring flowers and bulbs. The chef puts pansy and violet blossoms to use as garnishes for this salad (edible flowers of any kind may be used in other seasons).

1 pound salad greens (a mixture of Bibb, romaine, spinach, radicchio, Boston, etc.), washed and spun dry
1 red bell pepper, seeded and cut in strips
2 bunches scallions, trimmed and sliced
1 1/2 cups mandarin orange sections
Orange Dressing (see recipe below)
Walnut pieces, for garnish
Julienne of fresh basil, for garnish

1. Combine the salad greens, red pepper, scallion, and orange sections in a large salad bowl or arrange on individual salad plates.

2. Toss with Orange Dressing (add gradually to avoid drenching the greens) and garnish with walnut pieces and basil.

Serves 10.

Orange Dressing

1/2 can (12 ounces) frozen orange juice concentrate, thawed
3/4 cup canola oil
1/2 cup rice wine vinegar
4 teaspoons dried basil leaves
3/4 teaspoon crushed fresh garlic
1/2 teaspoon freshly ground pepper
1 dash Tabasco sauce

Combine all the ingredients in a jar with a lid and shake well to blend (or whisk together in a bowl).

Makes 2 cups.

Will's Sunday Salad with Tofu Dressing

THE INN AT STARLIGHT LAKE, STARLIGHT,
PENNSYLVANIA

Innkeeper Judith McMahon shares this recipe created by her son, Will McMahon, a professional skier and rock climber. He likes healthful but tasty meals—and this salad is a meal in itself. The ingredients may be varied to include other vegetables and nuts, and a different dressing may be substituted by those who aren't quite sure about tofu.

1/2 head romaine lettuce

5 ounces cold cooked spaghetti or other pasta

1/4 cup raisins

1/4 cup shredded carrot

1/2 cup Cheddar cheese cubes

1/4 cup broccoli flowerets

1/4 cup sliced fresh mushrooms

1/4 cup pine nuts

1 to 11/2 cups Tofu Dressing (see recipe below)

Place all the ingredients except the dressing in a bowl and mix well. Gradually add the Tofu Dressing until the mixture binds well. Serve cold.

Serves 4.

Tofu Dressing

6 ounces soft or medium soft tofu, blanched and crumbled

6 fresh spinach leaves, washed well and patted dry with paper towels

1 scallion, trimmed and chopped

1/4 green bell pepper, seeded and chopped

3 tablespoons cider vinegar

1 tablespoon chopped fresh basil or 1 teaspoon dried basil leaves

3/4 teaspoon salt

1/4 teaspoon freshly ground black pepper

1/2 cup water

1 cup vegetable oil

1. Place all the ingredients except the oil in a blender or the bowl of a food processor and blend until liquified.

2. With the machine running, drizzle in a steady stream of oil until the dressing thickens. Use immediately or store, covered, in the refrigerator for up to a week.

Makes about 1 3/4 cups.

Fiesta Salad

RANCHO DE LOS CABALLEROS, WICKENBURG, ARIZONA

The proprietors of Rancho de los Caballeros make it clear that caballeros were the gentlemen on horseback who explored and settled the Southwest—not to be confused with cowboys, bronco-busters, or ranch hands. The caballero's appreciation for skillful riding and well-bred horses as well as gracious living is the impetus for this comfortable and authentic guest ranch.

6 cups torn salad greens

1/4 cup freshly grated Parmesan cheese

6 slices bacon, cooked, drained well on paper towels, and crumbled

1 6-ounce jar artichoke hearts, drained and quartered

1 tomato, peeled, seeded, and chopped

2 cups salsa, commercial or homemade

1 cup commercial Ranch dressing

1. Combine the salad greens, Parmesan cheese, bacon, artichoke hearts and tomato in a large bowl.

2. Place the salsa in a blender and blend until smooth. Add the ranch dressing and blend to mix thoroughly.

3. Toss the salad and serve the dressing on the side.

Serves 6.

Mediterranean Fusilli Salad

TURNING POINT INN, FREDERICK, MARYLAND

Lunch service is something of a rarity at country inns, but Turning Point Inn is an exception. Tuesday through Friday, lunch is served not only to houseguests but to the public. This pasta salad, a hearty variation on the theme of salade niçoise *is a popular entrée.*

1 cup sun-dried tomatoes

1/4 cup red wine

1 pound fusilli or other heavy pasta, cooked

1/4 cup extra virgin olive oil

6 garlic cloves, roasted and diced (see note below)

4 tablespoons drained capers

1/2 cup white tuna, drained and flaked

1/2 cup chopped calamata olives

1/4 cup toasted pine nuts

2 ounces chèvre (goat cheese), crumbled

1. Marinate the sun-dried tomatoes for 2 hours in the red wine. Drain, reserving the wine for other cooking projects. Roughly chop the tomatoes.

2. Toss the sun-dried tomato with the remaining ingredients, except the chèvre, until thoroughly mixed. Top with the crumbled chèvre and serve.

Serves 6 to 8.

Note: To roast garlic, start with a whole head or individual unpeeled cloves. Wrap in aluminum foil and bake in an oven or toaster oven at 350 degrees F for 45 minutes to 1 hour, until soft. It will be easy to squeeze the roasted garlic out of the skins.

Harbor House Tabouleh

HARBOR HOUSE, ELK, CALIFORNIA

Harbor House advertises garden fresh cuisine, and this recipe provides an opportunity to make use of whatever your own garden offers. Among the optional ingredients are several items not usually associated with tabouleh—a nice change from the confines of the packaged version.

2 cups boiling water

2½ cups bulgur wheat

1 cup soy oil or light salad oil

½ cup Tamari (soy sauce)

1 cup fresh lemon juice

3 cucumbers, peeled, seeded, and finely diced

½ cup minced scallion

4 carrots, peeled and grated

½ cup chopped fresh parsley

Chopped fresh mint, diced celery, grated red cabbage, chopped red onions, chopped bell peppers, grated lemon rind, chopped tomatoes, chopped olives (optional)

1. In a large bowl, pour the boiling water over the bulgur wheat and let stand until the water has been absorbed. Chill.

2. Whisk together the oil, Tamari, and lemon juice.

3. Add to the bulgur the cucumber, scallion, carrots, parsley, and as many optional ingredients as you care to add. Gradually stir in the dressing. Cover and refrigerate for at least 2 hours before serving.

Serves 8 to 10.

Meat and Poultry Entrées

Meat and Poultry Entrées

Black Angus Strip Steak with Sherry–Mustard–Butter Sauce
Steak au Poivre
West Indian Rum Beef Stew
German Beef Roulade
Veal Provençale
Soya and Ginger Marinated Loin of Salt Spring Lamb
Rack of Lamb with Mustard and Herb Crust
Curried Lamb Stew
Grilled Lamb Rib Chops with Pear–Ginger Chutney
Pork Tenderloin with Cassis and Black Currants
Pork Tenderloin with an Ale and Cheddar Cheese Sauce
Stuffed Pork Loin with Apricots and Prunes
Grilled New Milford Pork Chops in a Honey Mustard Marinade
Pork Medallions with Pink Peppercorn Sauce
Venison Stew
Honey–Baked Rabbit
Chicken Chèvre Pâtisserie
Pecan–Breaded Breast of Chicken
Watercress Chicken
Chicken Brie
Linguine Michelangelo
Breast of Brome Lake Duckling with Wild Brambleberry
   and Spruce Jelly
Southwest Stuffed Quail with Black Beans and Spaghetti Squash
Roast Baby Quail Stuffed with Apricot Sausage

Black Angus Strip Steak with Sherry-Mustard-Butter Sauce

THE INN AT MONTPELIER, MONTPELIER, VERMONT

The two Federal Period mansions that form the inn are part of a row of nineteenth-century town houses in Montpelier's National Historic District. Restored from their most recent incarnations as apartments, the guest rooms and common rooms are handsomely furnished with period reproductions and antiques. Each house has a guest pantry where morning coffee and rolls are available for early (or late) risers, and a variety of refreshments are available throughout the day.

3 tablespoons butter, melted
6 8-ounce strip steaks, trimmed of all fat
Salt and freshly ground pepper to taste
1/2 cup finely chopped shallots
3 cloves garlic, minced
1 cup dry sherry
3 tablespoons sherry vinegar
1 teaspoon green peppercorns
1/4 cup heavy cream
2 tablespoons prepared whole grain mustard
3/4 cup (1 1/2 sticks) cold unsalted butter

1. Preheat a large heavy skillet over medium-high heat. Brush the melted butter on the steak and season with salt and pepper.

2. Sauté the steaks in batches, three at a time, about 2 minutes per side. Transfer to a warm plate.

3. In the same skillet, place the shallots, garlic, sherry, sherry vinegar, and green peppercorns and cook over medium-high heat until the liquids have reduced to about 2 tablespoons.

4. Add the cream and mustard and bring to a boil. Reduce the heat to low and whisk in the cold butter until just melted. Transfer the steaks to individual plates and spoon the sauce over them.

Serves 6.

Steak au Poivre

THE VERMONT INN, KILLINGTON, VERMONT

The Vermont Inn and Executive Chef Stephen Hatch have won the Killington Champagne Fine Dining contest for three consecutive years, and everything the kitchen produces is homemade, including the famous herb rolls. The menu features New England and Continental cuisine, and this popular dish is almost always on it.

4 10-ounce Delmonico center-cut steaks
1 cup freshly cracked pepper
1/4 cup brandy
2 tablespoons red wine vinegar
2 tablespoons Dijon mustard
2 tablespoons red currant jelly
2 dashes Tabasco sauce
2 cups Brown Sauce (your favorite recipe, or see page 99)

1. Lightly coat the outside edges of the steaks with cracked pepper.

2. Brown the steaks on both sides in a large, lightly salted preheated sauté pan (the timing depends on how rare you wish the steaks to be).

3. Remove the steaks from the pan and deglaze the pan with the brandy. Add the vinegar, mustard, jelly, Tabasco, and Brown Sauce. Heat, stirring, until the jelly is dissolved, and pour over the steaks.

Serves 4.

West Indian Rum Beef Stew

EAGLES MERE INN, EAGLES MERE, PENNSYLVANIA

Susan and Peter Glaubitz both had careers in three- and four-star restaurants before becoming innkeepers in 1991. Their sophisticated menu, which changes daily, reflects their background. At Eagles Mere, this stew is served in individual whole wheat bread boats. Small loaves of bread are made from thawed frozen dough, then hollowed out and dried in the oven before the "cargo" is added.

4 cups coarsely chopped onion

2 pounds prime rib of beef, roasted to medium rare, trimmed of fat and gristle and cut in 3/4-inch cubes (or roast pork or lamb)

1 green bell pepper, seeded and cut in 1/4-inch julienne

1 red bell pepper, seeded and cut in 1/4-inch julienne

1 yellow bell pepper, seeded and cut in 1/4-inch julienne

2 fresh tomatoes, coarsely chopped

2 teaspoons pressed garlic

1 tablespoon sugar

1 teaspoon freshly ground pepper

1 bay leaf, crumbled

1 cup water

1/3 cup tomato paste

1 teaspoon Tabasco sauce

1 teaspoon Vietnamese Sauce (available in shops carrying oriental foods)

1/3 cup stuffed olives

1/4 cup Myers's dark rum

1. Preheat the oven to 325 degrees F. Grease a baking pan.

2. Layer the onion, beef cubes, peppers, and tomatoes in the baking pan and sprinkle with the garlic, sugar, ground pepper, and bay leaf.

3. Combine the water, tomato paste, Tabasco, and Vietnamese Sauce in a small bowl and pour over the ingredients in the pan. Cover and bake for 35 minutes.

4. Remove from the oven and stir in the olives and rum.

Serves 6.

German Beef Roulade

THE LODGE AT LAKE CLEAR, LAKE CLEAR, NEW YORK

This 125-year-old Great Woods lodge combines the German heritage of the Hohmeyer family, innkeepers since 1965, and the rustic craftsmanship of Adirondack antiques and artifacts. The food, prepared by owner/chef Cathy Hohmeyer, is a unique blend of Old World tradition and seasonal Adirondack tastes. Cathy advises that though these roulades are time-consuming to assemble, they are a great make-ahead dish, since after being cooked they can sit for quite a while in the sauce over low heat. The toothpicks remain, so be sure to warn your guests.

1 5-pound boneless top round of beef (in one piece)

Salt and freshly ground pepper to taste

1 onion, coarsely chopped

8 to 10 dill pickle slices, or pieces

1/4 pound bacon, coarsely chopped, uncooked

Round wooden toothpicks

2 stalks celery, cut in pieces

2 carrots, cut in pieces

1 leek, white part only, cleaned and cut in pieces

1 bay leaf

2 tablespoons tomato paste

1/4 cup all-purpose flour

1 cup water

1/2 cup red wine

1. Preheat the oven to 350 degrees F.

2. Slice the roast into thin slices, obtaining the largest slices you can (an electric meat slicer works best for this).

3. For each roulade, lay 2 or 3 large slices on a cutting board, overlapping each other by half. Top with 1 or 2 of the smaller slices. Using the side of a meat cleaver, pound the pieces together where they join and until the entire surface is slightly flattened. Sprinkle with salt and pepper. Repeat until you have 8 large pieces.

4. In the center of each piece place some chopped onion, a pickle slice, and some chopped bacon. Fold down the top, then fold in the sides, and roll. Secure the finished roll with a toothpick at each end.

5. Place the roulades in a small roasting pan and add water so that the meat is three-quarters covered. Add the celery, carrots, leek, bay leaf, and tomato paste, and stir. Bake for 2½ hours, turning the roulades every half-hour.

6. Remove the roulades from the pan and pour off and strain the juice. (If time allows, chill the juice until any fat solidifies on the surface and remove the fat.)

7. Combine the flour and water to form a thin mixture, making sure there are no lumps. Bring the juices to a boil in a saucepan, and gradually stir in the flour and water mixture, continuing to cook over medium heat until the juices thicken (prepare more flour and water mixture if you wish a thicker sauce). Simmer for 10 minutes, season with salt and pepper, remove from the heat, and stir in the red wine.

8. Before serving, return the roulades to the pan with the sauce and reheat over low heat.

Serves 6 to 8.

Veal Provençale

ASA RANSOM HOUSE, CLARENCE, NEW YORK

Asa Ransom was a silversmith plying his trade in the small fur trading post on Lake Erie now known as Clarence. In 1799 he built a combination log home and tavern on the land the inn now occupies and during the next five years added a sawmill and a gristmill. The ruins of the gristmill still stand, and the oldest part of the present inn building dates from 1853. Two dining rooms added in 1975 blend perfectly and offer a choice of country formal or country rustic ambience.

1 pound veal medallions (or enough to make 3 per person)
All-purpose flour, for dredging
Olive oil
1 clove garlic, minced
1/2 cup white wine
2 scallions, chopped
1/4 cup chopped black olives
1 cup diced fresh tomatoes
1/2 cup tomato sauce

1. Dredge the veal medallions in flour, shaking off the excess.

2. Heat the olive oil in a sauté pan and sauté the medallions until golden on both sides. Pour off any excess oil.

3. Add the garlic and wine, heat to warm, and add the scallions, olives, tomatoes, and tomato sauce. Cook until the sauce is heated through and thickened. Serve immediately.

Serves 4.

Soya and Ginger Marinated Loin of Salt Spring Lamb

**HASTINGS HOUSE COUNTRY INN,
SALT SPRING ISLAND, BRITISH COLUMBIA**

Salt Spring Island is part of the Gulf Islands and can be reached by air, boat, or car ferry from Vancouver or Victoria. The terrain offers meadows, woodland, and seacoast, and local lamb and seafood are regularly part of the menu at Hastings House. This dish is served year-round, with whatever vegetable is available from the estate's garden and potatoes roasted with garlic.

7 tablespoons soy sauce

3 tablespoons olive oil

4 tablespoons grated ginger root

2 teaspoons crushed black peppercorns

4 teaspoons light brown sugar

4 teaspoons minced garlic

2 cups white wine

1 2½-pound boneless lamb loin, trimmed of all fat and sinew

1. Combine the soy sauce, olive oil, ginger, crushed peppercorns, brown sugar, garlic, and white wine. Place the lamb in a shallow dish, cover with the marinade, cover, and refrigerate for 6 to 12 hours.

2. Preheat the oven to 425 degrees F.

3. Remove the lamb from the dish, drain well, and pat dry.

4. Sear the lamb in a moderately hot pan on top of the stove until browned on all sides.

5. Roast for 10 to 15 minutes (depending on the diameter of the loin) or until medium rare. Slice and serve.

Serves 8.

Rack of Lamb with Mustard and Herb Crust

COBBLE HOUSE INN, GAYSVILLE, VERMONT

Guests are always welcome in the kitchen at the Cobble House, and Beau Benson doesn't mind being observed at work. She cooks by smell and taste and, unless she is baking, seldom measures anything. In this recipe, she stipulates that the bread crumbs and the herbs must be fresh, not dried. "Remember, it's the little things that count."

4 racks lamb, French trimmed and cut into 4 2-bone chops
Mustard and Herb Spread (see recipe below)
1 cup fresh French bread crumbs
2 tablespoons butter, melted

1. Preheat the oven to 450 degrees F. Grease a baking sheet with sides.

2. Brush the top and sides of the lamb chops with the Mustard and Herb Spread and roll the chops in the bread crumbs.

3. Place the chops on the prepared baking sheet and drizzle melted butter over the tops of the chops to help them brown. Bake 15 minutes for medium rare.

    Serves 4 generously.

Mustard and Herb Spread

2 cups strong Dijon mustard
2 tablespoons minced shallots
2 cloves garlic, minced
1 bunch fresh basil, chopped
2 tablespoons chopped fresh parsley

To make the Mustard and Herb Spread, combine all the ingredients in a bowl and transfer to a canning jar. Cover and refrigerate until ready to use.

Makes about 2 1/2 cups.

Note: The Mustard and Herb Spread keeps, refrigerated, for up to six months. It can be used as a coating for salmon, in salad dressings, and most any time you reach for mustard. To make a smaller quantity, cut the recipe in half.

Curried Lamb Stew

UNDER MOUNTAIN INN, SALISBURY, CONNECTICUT

British innkeeper/chef Peter Higginson pays his respects to the Commonwealth in this recipe, as he does in much of his cooking. Many of the special weekend packages that attract guests to this cozy inn in the Litchfield Hills of northwest Connecticut also have a decidedly British theme—Olde English Christmas, Dickens Weekend, and St. David's Day Celebration, to name a few.

3/4 cup (1 1/2 sticks) butter

4 large onions, minced

4 Granny Smith apples, unpeeled but cored and finely chopped

4 teaspoons curry powder

2 teaspoons ground ginger

2 teaspoons chili powder

2 teaspoons freshly ground pepper

1/4 teaspoon ground cloves

6 tablespoons tomato paste

5 pounds roasted lamb, cut in 1-inch cubes

6 cups chicken broth, or more, to cover meat

2 cups raisins

3 tablespoons cornstarch mixed with 1/2 cup water (optional)

1. In a frying pan, melt the butter and lightly sauté the onions and apples until soft but not brown. Stir in the curry powder, ginger, chili powder, pepper, cloves, and tomato paste.

2. Add the lamb, broth, and raisins and stir well. Simmer, uncovered, for 1 hour, skimming off any fat that floats to the top during the first half hour. If necessary, thicken with the cornstarch mixture 10 minutes before serving time.

Serves 8.

Grilled Lamb Rib Chops with Pear-Ginger Chutney

THE WHITE HART, SALISBURY, CONNECTICUT

Northwest Connecticut is still a somewhat well-kept secret. In summer, from the wicker and flower-bedecked front porch of the White Hart at one end of the green there is a perfect view of one of the prettiest towns in the region. Terry and Juliet Moore have given the historic inn a total makeover and invite guests for meetings, parties, or private getaways—"a quiet night, a spot near the fireplace, a lunch on the porch, a dance at the ball."

1/2 cup orange juice
3 tablespoons chili powder
1/2 teaspoon ground cinnamon
Pinch of ground mace
1 cup canola oil
12 rib lamb chops
Pear-Ginger Chutney (see recipe below)

1. Combine the orange juice, chili powder, cinnamon, and mace in a shallow dish large enough to hold the lamb chops in one layer and slowly whisk in the oil. Completely immerse the lamb chops in the marinade and refrigerate, covered, for 3 to 4 hours.

2. Grill the chops to the desired doneness and serve with a generous portion of the Pear-Ginger Chutney.

Serves 6.

Pear-Ginger Chutney

2 tablespoons canola oil
1/2 cup diced Spanish onion
2 tablespoons finely grated ginger root
1 dried red chili pod, seeded and crushed, or 1 tablespoon chili powder
1/4 cup dark brown sugar
1/4 cup cider vinegar
4 Bosc pears, peeled, cored, and cut in 1/2-inch dice
1 teaspoon freshly ground pepper

1/2 teaspoon ground cinnamon
1/2 teaspoon ground nutmeg
Pinch of ground clove

1. Place the canola oil in a sauté pan and add the onion, ginger, and chili. Sauté until the onion is soft but not brown. Add the brown sugar and continue cooking until the liquid caramelizes.

2. Add the vinegar, pears, and spices. Simmer over low heat until the pears have softened, 10 to 15 minutes.

Note: For adventurous diners, the amounts of chili in both the marinade and the chutney may be increased.

Pork Tenderloin with Cassis and Black Currants

PINE CREST INN, TRYON, NORTH CAROLINA

Here is one of the most popular dishes served at Pine Crest Inn. The slightly sweet sauce is a good match for the subtle flavor of pork. If you can't find dried black currants, raisins may be substituted.

4 tablespoons clarified butter or vegetable oil (see note below)

3 pounds pork tenderloins, trimmed

Salt and freshly ground pepper to taste

3 to 4 tablespoons dried black currants, soaked in warm water for
    30 minutes

3 tablespoons balsamic vinegar

4 ounces cassis liqueur

1 cup veal or chicken stock

6 tablespoons butter, at room temperature

1. Preheat the oven to 375 degrees F.

2. In a large skillet, heat the clarified butter over medium-high heat. Season the pork loins with salt and pepper and brown slightly on all sides (4 to 6 minutes).

3. Transfer the pork to an ovenproof dish and bake, uncovered, for 15 minutes (overcooking tends to dry out the meat).

4. Pour the excess butter from the skillet. Add the currants, vinegar, and cassis and bring to a boil over medium heat, scraping to dissolve any brown bits. Cook until the liquid is reduced by half.

5. Add the stock and again reduce by half. Whisk in the butter, 1 tablespoon at a time, until the sauce thickens.

6. Remove the pork from the oven and let stand about 10 minutes. To serve, slice the pork into 1/2-inch slices, arrange on individual plates, and spoon the sauce over the slices.

Serves 6 to 8.

Note: Clarified butter is made by melting butter over low heat and pouring off the yellow liquid, leaving the milky residue in the pan to be discarded. The yellow liquid is the clarified butter.

Pork Tenderloin with an Ale and Cheddar Cheese Sauce

SWIFT HOUSE INN, MIDDLEBURY, VERMONT

Cherry paneling, Chippendale chairs, starched white linens, and candlelight combine to produce an elegant atmosphere for fine dining at Swift House. This simple dish is one of the inn's most popular and is served with a seasonal fruit garnish—poached pears, crab apples, or a chutney.

4 6-ounce pork tenderloins
Salt and freshly ground pepper to taste
Oil for sautéing
1 bottle good quality ale or beer
1 shallot, minced
1 clove garlic, minced
1/2 cup heavy cream
2 cups good quality beef broth
1/2 cup grated extra sharp Cheddar cheese

1. Preheat the oven to 400 degrees F.

2. Season the pork with salt and pepper. Place a small amount of oil in a sauté pan and heat until it is hot but not smoking. Add the tenderloins and brown on all sides.

3. Transfer the tenderloins to a baking sheet and bake to the desired doneness (10 to 15 minutes), leaving the meat slightly pink. Remove the meat to a platter and keep warm.

4. Add the ale, shallot, garlic, cream, and beef broth to the sauté pan. Reduce over high heat until only 1 cup liquid remains. Lower the heat, whisk in the cheese, and blend until smooth.

5. Slice the tenderloins, place on individual plates, and spoon the sauce over the meat.

Serves 4.

Stuffed Pork Loin with Apricots and Prunes

THE INN AT STARLIGHT LAKE, STARLIGHT, PENNSYLVANIA

This recipe, an excellent choice for a holiday menu, can be prepared the day before and baked just before serving. At the Inn at Starlight Lake, the pork loin is often served with baked stuffed potatoes and julienne green beans with toasted almonds.

1 3- to 4-pound boneless pork loin
6 ounces sun-dried apricots
6 ounces pitted prunes
Fruit Glaze (see recipe below)

1. Preheat the oven to 325 degrees F. Cover the bottom of a baking pan with aluminum foil.

2. Butterfly the pork loin. Use a meat tenderizing device to flatten the meat until it is approximately 1/2 inch thick.

3. Boil the apricots and prunes in water to cover for 5 minutes. Strain, reserving the liquid.

4. Purée the fruit in a blender or food processor until smooth. You will need half of the purée for stuffing the loin and the other half for the Fruit Glaze.

5. Spread the puréed fruit over the meat. Roll the loin lengthwise into a tight roll. Tie in several places with butcher's string. (Recipe may be prepared in advance to this point.)

6. Place the pork on the prepared baking pan and bake for 1 1/2 hours, or until the internal temperature is 180 degrees F. Cut the loin in slices 1/4 to 1/2 inch thick. Pour some of the warmed Fruit Glaze over the slices.

Fruit Glaze

3/4 cup pineapple juice
3/4 cup apple juice
1 cup reserved liquid from cooking apricots and prunes
1/2 cup water
1 tablespoon cornstarch
1/2 fruit purée (see instruction 4, above)

1. Place the pineapple juice, apple juice, and reserved cooking liquid in a saucepan. Combine the water and the cornstarch and stir into the juices. Heat over medium heat until the sauce thickens.

2. Stir in the purée and heat, stirring.

Serves 4 to 6.

Grilled New Milford Pork Chops in a Honey Mustard Marinade

THE GRISWOLD INN, ESSEX, CONNECTICUT

The public spaces at country inns are often graced with the innkeeper's prized collections—at the Griswold Inn there are myriad Currier and Ives steamboat prints, a collection of firearms dating from the fifteenth century, and a historic collection of Antonio Jacobsen marine art.

8 pork loin chops, 3/4 inch thick
1/2 cup apple cider
6 cloves garlic, crushed
1/2 onion, diced
1/2 cup salad oil
2 teaspoons freshly ground pepper
2 tablespoons Dijon mustard
2 tablespoons honey
1 teaspoon rosemary

1. Place the pork chops in a container deep enough to hold them in one layer, covered with the marinade.

2. To make the marinade, combine the remaining ingredients in a medium bowl. Pour half of the mixture over the pork chops. Turn the chops over and pour over the rest of the marinade. Cover and refrigerate for at least 4 hours, turning the chops every hour.

3. Prepare a grill or preheat a broiler. Drain the pork chops, reserving the marinade, and grill or broil them for 5 to 7 minutes per side, brushing with the reserved marinade.

Serves 4.

Pork Medallions with Pink Peppercorn Sauce

SCHUMACHER'S NEW PRAGUE HOTEL, NEW PRAGUE, MINNESOTA

Owner/chef John Schumacher graduated from the Culinary Institute of America with high honors and is a teacher himself. His one-day seminars range from Introduction to a Culinary Career to Children's Introduction to Cooking, which he teaches with his mother, Grandma Schu. Shumacher and his hotel have garnered a long list of awards, including National Pork Restaurant of the Year.

1 pound boneless pork loin, sliced into 12 thin slices
1 cup all-purpose flour, seasoned with salt and pepper
1/4 cup clarified butter (see note page 94)
1/3 cup minced shallots
1 tablespoon fresh lemon juice
1 1/2 cups Brown Sauce (see recipe below)
1 cup dry white wine
2 teaspoons pink peppercorns
1/2 teaspoon salt
1/4 teaspoon freshly ground pepper
2 teaspoons parsley flakes

1. Flatten the pork slices with a mallet and dredge in the seasoned flour.

2. Heat the clarified butter in a large sauté pan until bubbling. Add the pork slices and shallots and sauté for 30 seconds, taking care not to let the shallots brown. Add the lemon juice, Brown Sauce, white wine, peppercorns, and salt and pepper.

3. Reduce the heat and simmer over low heat for 15 minutes, gently stirring occasionally.

4. Add the parsley flakes, add more white wine to adjust the consistency of the sauce if necessary, bring to a boil, and serve.

Serves 4.

Note: This recipe may also be used with veal or skinless, boneless chicken breasts.

Brown Sauce

6 tablespoons (3/4 stick) butter or margarine
1 cup diced onion
1/2 cup diced celery
1/2 cup diced carrot
6 tablespoons all-purpose flour
6 cups beef stock, double strength
1/4 cup tomato purée
1 bay leaf
1 teaspoon salt
1/4 teaspoon freshly ground pepper

1. In a heavy saucepan, heat the butter until bubbling and sauté the vegetables until the onions are translucent. Add the flour and cook for 2 minutes over low heat, stirring frequently with a wooden spoon or rubber spatula.

2. Heat the stock and gradually add it to the vegetable mixture, stirring constantly. (To make double-strength stock, reduce 12 cups of beef stock to 6 cups by boiling rapidly. Canned broth or consommé may be substituted for homemade stock.)

3. Add the tomato purée, bay leaf, and salt and pepper, and cook for 30 minutes. Adjust the flavor and consistency to taste. Strain.

Makes 6 cups.

Note: The sauce freezes well and may be frozen in 1-cup amounts in freezer bags for future use.

Venison Stew

LAKE PLACID LODGE, LAKE PLACID, NEW YORK

David and Christie Garrett bought the former Lake Placid Manor in 1993 and reopened it, completely refurbished, in July 1994. Situated on the wooded shore of Lake Placid, in the shadow of Whiteface Mountain, the hotel is a vintage Adirondack lodge of birch branches, painted pine, and diamond-paned windows. The rustic but comfortable rooms are furnished with pieces created by local artisans. The restaurant advertises sophisticated French-American cuisine with an Adirondack flair—or, as one reviewer has said, "Adirondack gourmet."

Vegetable oil
3 pounds lean venison stewing meat, trimmed and cut in 1/4-inch cubes
4 large onions, chopped
6 large carrots, chopped
3 stalks celery, chopped
3 leeks, well cleaned and chopped
1 whole head garlic, peeled and minced
1 bunch fresh thyme, chopped
1 bottle red wine
2 1/2 quarts veal stock, if available, or half beef, half chicken stock
Chopped fresh thyme, for finishing
Salt and freshly ground pepper to taste

1. Preheat the oven to 300 degrees F.

2. Heat a sauté pan, coat with a small amount of vegetable oil, and sear the venison until it reaches a dark color. Transfer the venison to a 6-quart braising dish.

3. Place the chopped vegetables and garlic in the sauté pan and cook over medium heat, stirring frequently, until the mixture is beginning to brown. Add to the braising dish with the chopped bunch of thyme.

4. Deglaze the sauté pan with the wine and reduce until the liquid has almost disappeared. Transfer the remaining liquid to the braising dish, and stir in the veal stock. Bring to a simmer on top of the stove, then cover and bake for 2 1/2 hours, or until tender.

5. Remove the dish from the oven, discard the vegetables, and strain off the sauce into a saucepan. Reduce the sauce by half to strengthen and improve the flavor.

6. Place the venison in the sauce to reheat and add the freshly chopped thyme and salt and pepper. Serve with potato purée and root vegetables, such as carrots, turnips, and parsnips.

Serves 8.

Honey-Baked Rabbit

THE ORCHARD INN, SALUDA, NORTH CAROLINA

Norman Simpson, originator of the Country Inns and Back Roads series, had this to say about the Orchard Inn: ". . . there are many words that come to my mind—flowers, paintings, music, the view, cordiality, intellectual curiosity, good conversation, mountain tranquillity, and the changing tones and colors as they are affected by the mists off the mountains at various times of the day." Much of this can be experienced from the dining room, an airy sunporch that stretches the length of the inn.

2 rabbits, dressed and cut up
1/2 cup (1 stick) butter, melted
1/2 cup honey
2 tablespoons prepared mustard
1 teaspoon salt
1 teaspoon freshly ground pepper
1 teaspoon curry powder
1/2 cup sherry

1. Preheat the oven to 350 degrees F.

2. Arrange the rabbit pieces in a shallow baking pan.

3. Combine the remaining ingredients in a small bowl and pour over the rabbit. Bake for 1 1/4 hours, basting frequently, until golden.

Serves 4.

Chicken Chèvre Pâtisserie

THE SQUIRE TARBOX INN, WISCASSET, MAINE

Innkeeper Karen Mitman recommends an experimental attitude toward this simple preparation. The cheese can be spiced with combinations such as garlic and chives, basil and oregano, rosemary and thyme, or with chopped sun-dried tomatoes—to name just a few possibilities.

4 boneless, skinless chicken breast halves (almost 6 ounces each), rinsed, patted dry, and pounded to 1/4-inch thickness

4 to 8 tablespoons chèvre (goat cheese), flavored with your choice of seasonings

4 puff pastry squares (5 to 6 inches square), cut from sheets of frozen puff pastry

Salt and freshly ground pepper to taste

1 egg, lightly beaten

1. Preheat the oven to 425 degrees F. Grease a baking sheet.

2. Place 1 or 2 tablespoons of chèvre in the center of each flattened breast and fold the chicken around the cheese.

3. Place a rolled breast half in the center of each pastry square and sprinkle with salt and pepper.

4. Pull the pastry up around the chicken to encase it. Pinch the seams together and seal with warm water. Place the pastry packages seam side down on the prepared baking sheet. Garnish the top of each package with a design cut from additional puff pastry if you wish.

5. Poke four holes in the top of each package and brush with the beaten egg. Bake for 25 minutes. Let stand for 10 minutes before serving.

Serves 4.

Pecan-Breaded Breast of Chicken

THE VILLAGE INN, LENOX, MASSACHUSETTS

Located right in the center of Lenox, the Village Inn is within easy walking distance of the town's enticing shops, galleries, antiques shops, historic buildings, and parks. The relatively fit will find Tanglewood (summer home to the Boston Symphony Orchestra) a manageable walking distance as well.

4 boneless, skinless chicken breast halves (from 8-ounce breasts)

Salt and white pepper to taste

All-purpose flour for dredging

1/2 cup coarsely chopped pecans

Clarified butter (see note page 94)

2 tablespoons minced shallots

1/4 cup white wine

2 tablespoons Dijon mustard

1/2 cup heavy cream

2 tablespoons butter

Juice from 1/2 lemon

1. Preheat the oven to 375 degrees F.

2. Season the chicken breasts with salt and pepper and dredge with flour, shaking to remove any excess. Set aside for 1 minute, or until the flour becomes sticky to the touch. Dredge in the chopped pecans.

3. Barely cover the bottom of a small sauté pan with an ovenproof handle with clarified butter. When it is hot and bubbling, add the chicken and sauté on each side until the pecans begin to brown.

4. Place the pan in the oven to allow the chicken to finish cooking, for 15 to 20 minutes.

5. Remove the cooked chicken from the pan and set aside, covering it to keep warm. Add the shallots, wine, and mustard to the pan and allow to cook briefly over medium heat. Add the cream and bring to a boil.

6. Swirl in the butter and add the lemon juice and more salt and pepper. Place the chicken breasts on individual plates and cover with the sauce.

Serves 2.

Watercress Chicken

THE BIRD & BOTTLE INN, GARRISON, NEW YORK

Warren's Tavern, now the Bird & Bottle, opened in 1761, and many of the building's original details are still in evidence. The dining room, known as the Warren Room, has early paneling, hand-hewn beams, and a large, denticulated fireplace.

1 boneless, skinless chicken breast, trimmed of all fat
1 egg white
1 1/4 cups heavy cream
Pinch of ground nutmeg
Pinch of salt
Pinch of cayenne pepper
1 bunch watercress, stems removed and chopped fine
6 boned chicken breast halves with wing bones left on (6 to 8 ounces each)
3 cups chicken broth
Watercress sprigs, for garnish

Sauce
1 small shallot, minced
1 tablespoon unsalted butter
1/2 cup white wine
1 cup chicken stock
1 3/4 cups heavy cream
2 tablespoons watercress, julienne cut
4 tablespoons diced tomatoes
Salt and freshly ground pepper to taste

1. Blend the chicken breast and egg white in a food processor until the mixture is smooth. Transfer to a bowl and chill for 30 minutes.

2. Preheat the oven to 375 degrees F.

3. Place the bowl of chicken mixture over a bed of ice and slowly stir in the heavy cream. Pass the mixture through a sieve. Season with the nutmeg, salt, and cayenne and fold in the watercress.

4. Remove the skin and fat from the chicken breast halves. Using a sharp knife with a narrow blade, put a hole down the center of the breast half, lengthwise, starting from the wing joint. Fill a pastry tube with the mousse and, using a plain tip, pipe the mousse into the hole. Repeat with the remaining breast halves.

5. Place the chicken in a roasting pan and pour the chicken broth over it. Cover the pan with aluminum foil and bake for 45 to 50 minutes.

6. To make the sauce, in a saucepan, sauté the shallot in the butter until it is soft but not brown, 3 to 4 minutes. Deglaze the pan with the wine, and reduce the mixture to 1/4 cup over high heat. Add the chicken stock and reduce to 1/2 cup.

7. Add the cream, bring to a boil, and simmer for 3 to 4 minutes. Add the watercress and tomatoes and salt and pepper.

8. Remove the chicken from the broth and place on warm individual plates. Surround the chicken breast with sauce and garnish with watercress sprigs.

Serves 6.

Note: You may substitute whole boneless chicken breasts for the breast halves with wing bones. Lightly flatten the breasts, place some mousse in the center of each, roll, and secure with toothpicks. Roast for 35 to 40 minutes.

Chicken Brie

COBBLE HOUSE INN, GAYSVILLE, VERMONT

*This deliciously rich dish was selected for **Woman's Day** magazine's Great American Cooks issue in December 1993 and is still a favorite at the Cobble House.*

8 boneless, skinless chicken breast halves (from 7-ounce breasts)
1/4 cup all-purpose flour
3 tablespoons butter
1 1/2 cups chicken broth
1/4 cup minced shallots
2 tablespoons fresh lemon juice
2 teaspoons minced garlic
1 14-ounce can artichoke hearts, drained and cut in half
1/4 cup chopped fresh basil
8 ounces Brie cheese, rind removed

1. Dredge the chicken breasts in flour, shaking to remove any excess. Heat the butter in a sauté pan and cook the breasts over high heat for 4 minutes, turning once.

2. Add the chicken broth, shallots, lemon juice, and garlic to the sauté pan and bring to a boil over high heat. Reduce to simmer and cook the chicken for 8 to 10 minutes, until the juices run clear and the sauce is reduced. (If the sauce reduces too quickly, lower the heat and add a little more broth.)

3. Transfer the chicken to a platter and keep warm.

4. Add the artichoke hearts and fresh basil to the sauce and cook over low heat until the artichoke hearts are warm. Remove the sauce from the stove.

5. Transfer the chicken to individual serving plates. Press a piece of Brie onto the top of each chicken breast and press it flat with your fingers, breaking it into pieces. Pour the sauce over the top and serve immediately. The heat of the sauce will soften and melt the Brie.

Serves 4.

Linguine Michelangelo

NORTH HERO HOUSE, NORTH HERO, VERMONT

North Hero is part of the chain of Champlain Islands, reached by causeway from Burlington, Vermont (as well as by bridge or ferry from other points), and the activities surrounding a stay at North Hero House represent the best of what the lake region has to offer—water sports, fishing, antiquing, golf, tennis, concerts, amateur theatricals, and a weekly auction. The inn is open from mid-May to mid-October.

1 pound linguine (or any other pasta, or rice)

4 tablespoons peanut or canola oil

2 slices ginger root (about the size of a quarter), peeled and minced

2 cloves garlic, minced

1 pound boneless, skinless chicken breasts, sliced 1/4 inch
  thick horizontally

12 jumbo shrimp, peeled and deveined

8 ounces fresh mushrooms, sliced 1/4 inch thick

6 ounces snow peas, strings removed

1 red bell pepper, in 1/4-inch julienne

2 cups hot chicken stock

6 tablespoons light soy sauce

Dash of white pepper

3 tablespoons cornstarch dissolved in 6 tablespoons water

1. Cook linguine al dente, drain, and toss with a small amount of vegetable oil to prevent it from clumping. Keep hot, covered.

2. In a large frying pan or a wok over medium-high heat, heat the oil until a drop of water sizzles. Add the ginger and garlic and cook for 20 seconds. Add the chicken, shrimp, and mushrooms and cook for 3 minutes, stirring frequently. Add the snow peas and red bell pepper; cook for 2 minutes, stirring frequently.

3. Add the chicken stock, soy sauce, and white pepper and raise the heat to high. When the mixture is near boiling, quickly stir in two-thirds of the cornstarch mixture. Stir, adding more cornstarch mixture if a thicker consistency is desired. Spoon over equal portions of hot linguine.

Serves 4.

Breast of Brome Lake Duckling with Wild Brambleberry and Spruce Jelly

HOVEY MANOR, NORTH HATLEY, QUEBEC

The most splendid of all the summer places at North Hatley was the Mount Vernon look-alike constructed in 1900 for George Atkinson, president of Georgia Power and Light. It is now the central building of Hovey Manor. Also on the grounds are the former servants' quarters, icehouse, pump house, electric house and caretaker's house—all converted for bedroom space. Many of the buildings contain antiques purchased by Henry Atkinson himself.

4 relatively lean duck breasts

Spruce Jelly

1 cup water

1 cup sugar

3 ounces spruce needles

Leek Confit

3/4 cup chopped leeks (white part only, well cleaned)

3 tablespoons butter, at room temperature

2 1/2 tablespoons sugar

2 tablespoons white vinegar

Sauce

1 shallot, minced

1 clove garlic, minced

1 1/2 tablespoons olive oil

2 tablespoons red wine vinegar

1/2 cup red wine

2/3 cup duck stock

1 cup fresh or frozen brambleberries (blackberries)

Salt and freshly ground pepper to taste

1. Prepare the spruce jelly a day ahead. Bring the water to a boil in a saucepan, then add the sugar and spruce needles. Reduce the volume by half over high heat, and strain out the needles. Let cool and refrigerate.

2. Make the leek confit a day ahead. Sauté the leeks in the butter in a small sauté pan until soft. Add the sugar and vinegar and cook over medium heat for 5 minutes. Cool and refrigerate.

3. Make the sauce by sautéing the shallot and garlic in olive oil in a sauté pan until golden (be careful not to burn). Deglaze the pan with the vinegar and wine. Add the duck stock and the berries. Cook over medium heat for 10 minutes, stirring occasionally. Push the sauce through a sieve and season with salt and pepper.

4. Preheat the oven to 375 degrees F.

5. Briefly cook the duck breasts either in a hot frying pan or over charcoal, with the fat side down. Place the breasts in a baking pan and finish cooking in the oven for 10 minutes, until pink but not cooked through.

6. To serve, thinly slice the duck and fan on warm individual plates. Drizzle the sauce around the duck and serve with a tablespoon of the spruce jelly and a tablespoon of the leek confit on each side of the duck. Garnish with seasonal fresh vegetables.

Serves 4.

Note: The sauce, spruce jelly, and leek confit all may be prepared up to three days ahead of time and refrigerated, leaving only the duck to prepare at the last minute.

Southwest Stuffed Quail with Black Beans and Spaghetti Squash

RANCHO DE LOS CABALLEROS, WICKENBURG, ARIZONA

The Gant family has owned Rancho de los Caballeros for nearly fifty years, and their warm western hospitality has kept families returning for several generations. An hour's drive northwest of Phoenix, the ranch offers golf, tennis, swimming, and, as might be expected, a top-notch corral. A healthy appetite is a basic requirement for guests, since the inn's American plan provides three substantial meals a day. This typical southwestern dish involves several steps (many happening simultaneously) and thinking ahead—since the beans need to be soaked overnight.

1/2 pound black beans, soaked overnight

8 ounces wild rice blend

1 pound beef chorizo

8 semi-boneless cleaned and dressed quail

1 spaghetti squash

1 tablespoon butter

Salt and freshly ground pepper to taste

2 tablespoons vegetable oil

1 cup diced onion

1/2 cup diced green chilies

Salt and freshly ground pepper to taste

1 quart beef stock

1/2 teaspoon cilantro

1/2 teaspoon chili powder

1/2 teaspoon garlic powder

1/4 teaspoon ground cumin

2 tablespoons roux, more or less (see note below)

Chopped fresh parsley, for garnish

1. Drain the beans, cover with fresh water, bring to a boil, and cook, covered, over low heat until tender, about 1 1/2 hours.

2. Cook the rice according to the instructions on the package. Set aside to cool.

3. Crumble the chorizo, removing it from any casing, and sauté in a frying pan over medium heat. Drain off the fat. Let cool.

4. Preheat the oven to 350 degrees F.

5. Combine well the rice and chorizo and stuff the quails. Set them in a baking pan and roast for 40 minutes.

6. Boil the spaghetti squash (unpeeled) in water to cover for about 30 minutes (or prick with a fork and microwave on high power for 20 minutes). Cut in half, remove the seeds, and fluff with a fork. Season with the butter and salt and pepper and keep warm.

7. Heat the oil and sauté the onion and green chilies, add salt and pepper, and combine with the black beans.

8. Bring the beef stock to a boil in a saucepan, and add the cilantro, chili powder, garlic powder, and cumin. Whisk in the roux and continue cooking, stirring constantly, until the sauce has thickened.

9. To serve, place the quail on a nest of squash and serve the black beans on the side. Pour the sauce over the quail and garnish with the parsley.

Serves 6 to 8.

Note: To make roux, melt 2 or more tablespoons of butter in a small frying pan and stir in an equal amount of flour. Cook, stirring, over low heat for 3 to 5 minutes.

Roast Baby Quail Stuffed with Apricot Sausage

FRIENDS LAKE INN, CHESTERTOWN, NEW YORK

*Innkeepers Sharon and Greg Taylor are wine connoisseurs, and Friends Lake Inn has been celebrated as an award-winning cellar by the **Wine Spectator** since 1991. Although their holdings range from basic to sublime, the Taylors take pride in providing an affordable list of high quality wines and make a point of pairing menu items with the appropriate choice of wine.*

4 ounces dried apricots, chopped

1 red onion, minced

1/8 teaspoon ground cloves

1/8 teaspoon ground nutmeg

1/4 teaspoon dried thyme leaves

1/4 teaspoon white pepper

1 teaspoon kosher salt

12 ounces ground pork (20 to 25 percent fat)

8 semi-boneless quail

4 strips bacon, cut in half

2 carrots, cut into sticks

2 celery stalks, cut into sticks

1 large onion, cut into strips

1 cup water

1. Preheat the oven to 450 degrees F.

2. Mix the apricots, red onion, clove, nutmeg, thyme, pepper, and salt with the ground pork.

3. Fill each quail cavity with an equal amount of the sausage mix and place a strip of bacon over the breast of each bird.

4. Spread the carrots, celery, and onions over the bottom of a roasting pan and place the quail on top. Pour in the water and bake for 20 to 25 minutes; the bacon will be crispy.

5. To serve, place two quail on each plate. Strain the juices from the bottom of the roasting pan, discarding the vegetables, and spoon over the quail. Accompany with Green Onion and Saffron Risotto (see page 71).

Serves 4.

Seafood Entrées

Seafood Entrées

Grilled Swordfish with Roasted Corn and Tomato Relish

Herb-Marinated Swordfish

Marinated Rockfish

Baked Fillet of Salmon Stuffed with Scallops and Mandarin Oranges

Grilled Salmon with Squaw Corn

Grilled Tahini-Marinated Caribbean Red Snapper with Mango Coulis

Oyster Pan Roast

Gingered Snapper

Pan-Seared Scallops with Pancetta, Leeks, and Fresh Oregano

Shrimp and Artichoke Romano

Shrimp and Crabmeat Casserole

Crab Imperial

Lobster Shiitake Crêpes

Bouillabaisse

Lobster Dublin Lawyer

Grilled Swordfish with Roasted Corn and Tomato Relish

BARROWS HOUSE, DORSET, VERMONT

At the Barrows House, heart-healthy dishes are starred on Chef Gary Walker's menu, and this summertime entrée is a favorite. Seasonal specialties are part of what keeps guests returning at all times of year. Food, scenery, activities, and special attractions all change with the season. A highlight in summer is the Littlest Music Festival, a series of concerts held on the lawn in June and July. Admission is by donation of nonperishable items for local food pantries.

4 6-ounce swordfish steaks

Relish

2 ears corn, roasted with husk on and then kernels removed from cob
2 tomatoes, peeled, seeded, and diced
1 clove garlic, minced
1 small jalapeño pepper, diced
1/2 small red onion, diced
1/2 small red bell pepper, diced
1 teaspoon ground cumin
1 teaspoon chili powder
1 teaspoon cayenne pepper
1 teaspoon minced fresh cilantro
1 tablespoon fresh lime juice
1 tablespoon Champagne vinegar
Salt and freshly ground pepper to taste

1. Prepare coals for grilling.

2. Combine all the ingredients for the relish and mix well. Season with salt and pepper.

3. Grill the swordfish to the desired doneness. Top with the relish and serve.

   Serves 4.

Herb-Marinated Swordfish

THE WATERFORD INNE, WATERFORD, MAINE

This recipe was given to Innkeeper Rosalie Vanderzanden by a former guest, and the dish has had rave reviews from all who have tried it—with many requests for the recipe. It has made swordfish lovers out of people who previously found it to be either too dry or too fishy.

1/2 cup olive oil
2 teaspoons crushed garlic
4 tablespoons fresh lemon juice
4 tablespoons soy sauce
2 tablespoons chopped fresh parsley
1 teaspoon dill weed
4 8-ounce swordfish steaks

1. Combine the olive oil, garlic, lemon juice, soy sauce, parsley, and dill weed.

2. Place the swordfish in a shallow dish, prick with a fork , and pour over the marinade. Let marinate, refrigerated, for 1 to 3 hours, turning several times.

3. Prepare coals for grilling.

4. Grill, turning once, for 4 minutes per side. Serve immediately.

Serves 4.

Marinated Rockfish

HARBOR HOUSE, ELK, CALIFORNIA

The carefully planned menu at Harbor House depends on wholesome foods from local sources—homegrown vegetables, naturally raised meats and cheeses from nearby farms, and fish from waters just off the inn's shore. Rockfish is a general term for fish that live among rocks or on rocky bottoms.

6 medium rockfish fillets
Salt and freshly ground pepper to taste
3/4 cup olive oil
1 tablespoon prepared mustard
1 tablespoon red wine vinegar
1 teaspoon bottled horseradish
1/2 teaspoon paprika
Pinch of curry powder
Pinch of cayenne pepper
1 teaspoon garlic juice
Bread crumbs
Lemon wedges, for garnish

1. Sprinkle the fillets with salt and pepper.

2. Combine the olive oil, mustard, vinegar, horseradish, paprika, curry powder, cayenne, and garlic juice. Marinate the fillets in the mixture for at least 1 hour.

3. Preheat the oven to 500 degrees F.

4. Remove the fillets from the marinade, reserving the marinade, coat with bread crumbs, and arrange on a rack in a broiling pan. Drizzle with the remaining marinade.

5. Broil for 4 minutes under a hot broiler, then place on the bottom shelf of the preheated oven for 5 minutes. Serve with lemon wedges.

Serves 6.

Note: Innkeeper Helen Turner's rule of thumb for cooking fish is 10 minutes of total cooking time for each inch of thickness.

Baked Fillet of Salmon Stuffed with Scallops and Mandarin Oranges

MONTAGUE INN, SAGINAW, MICHIGAN

Truly a full-service establishment, Montague Inn serves breakfast, lunch, and dinner, with a complimentary breakfast buffet for overnight guests. The sunny dining room is transformed by candlelight in the evening, with a list of vintage wines to accompany the chef's fine menu.

6 ounces sea scallops, diced

3 ounces mandarin orange sections, diced

1 tablespoon chopped fresh herbs, preferably a mixture of tarragon, chives, and dill

4 salmon fillets, approximately 7 ounces each

1/4 cup fresh lemon juice

1/4 cup white wine

Salt and freshly ground pepper to taste

Slices of Pineapple Butter (see recipe below)

1. Preheat the oven to 400 degrees F. Butter a shallow baking dish.

2. Prepare the stuffing by mixing together the scallops, oranges, and herbs.

3. Slice a pocket into the side of each salmon fillet, divide the stuffing among the pockets, and place the salmon in the prepared baking dish.

4. Pour over the salmon the lemon juice, wine, and salt and pepper and bake for 15 minutes. Serve with a slice of Pineapple Butter.

Serves 4.

Pineapple Butter

1/2 cup (1 stick) unsalted butter, at room temperature

2 tablespoons finely minced pineapple

1 teaspoon fresh lemon juice

Combine all the ingredients and mix well. Form into a cylinder, wrap in plastic wrap, and chill. Cut in 1/2-inch slices.

Philbrook Farm Dark Bread, Philbrook Farm Inn, Shelburne, New Hampshire.

*Village Inn Scones.
The Village Inn, Lenox,
Massachusetts.*

CRAIG HAMMELL

*Sticky Buns.
Captain Lord
Mansion,
Kennebunkport,
Maine.*

CRAIG HAMMELL

Raspberry Chocolate Chip Muffins. Sea Crest by the Sea, Spring Lake, New Jersey.

Chocolate Lovers' French Toast. The Inn at Harbor Head, Kennebunkport, Maine.

Cassolette d'Escargots. The Homestead Inn, Greenwich, Connecticut.

Corner bedroom at the Hancock Inn, Hancock, New Hampshire.

Pumpkin Soup (blue and white tureen), among offerings at the Old Tavern at Grafton, Vermont.

CRAIG HAMMELL

Chilled Zucchini Bisque with Chesapeake Crab and Roasted Pepper (shown here with braised loin of pork). Turning Point Inn, Frederick, Maryland.

CRAIG HAMMELL

Gazpacho. The Sherwood Inn, Skaneateles, New York.

CRAIG HAMMELL

Soups from the Griswold Inn, Essex, Connecticut. Included in this book: Seafood Asparagus Chowder (bottom) and Oyster Stew with Winter Vegetables (right).

A feast from the Nathaniel Porter Inn, Warren, Rhode Island. Included in this book: Scallops with Roasted Red Pepper, Leeks, and Lemon Butter (far right) and Crème Brulée (center).

CRAIG HAMMELL

Pan-Seared Scallops with Pancetta, Leeks, and Fresh Oregano and Mediterranean Fusilli Salad. The Turning Point Inn, Frederick, Maryland.

CRAIG HAMMELL

Bounty from the Three Village Inn, Stony Brook, Long Island. Included in this book: Cold Plum Soup (upper right) and Corn Chowder with Peconic Bay Scallops (lower left).

Wines of the Inn on the Common, Craftsbury Common, Vermont.

Dishes with chèvre supplied by the resident goats of the Squire Tarbox Inn in Wiscasset, Maine. Spinach and Chèvre Tart (center left), Chèvre Pound Cake (center right), Chicken Chèvre Pâtisserie (foreground).

At the Cobble House Inn in Gaysville, Vermont, both lamb and salmon are prepared with a mustard and herb crust. The lamb recipe is included in this book.

COURTESY THE COBBLE HOUSE INN

CRAIG HAMMELL

Lobster Shiitake Crêpes. The Red Lion Inn, Stockbridge, Massachusets.

Lobster Dublin Lawyer. Dockside Guest Quarters, York, Maine.

Red Lion Inn Cranberry
Apple Crisp.
The Red Lion Inn,
Stockbridge, Massachusetts.

CRAIG HAMMELL

*At the White
Hart, Salisbury,
Connecticut, a side
dish with two house
specialties: Grilled
Lamb Rib Chops
with Pear–
Ginger Chutney
(foreground) and
Terrine of Grilled
Vegetables and
Goat Cheese
(center right).*

CRAIG HAMMELL

Warm French Bread Pudding. The Cobble House Inn, Gaysville, Vermont.

CRAIG HAMMELL

Chocolate Orange Drizzle Cake. Captain's House Inn, Chatham, Massachusetts.

CRAIG HAMMELL

Sugar Cone with Crème Anglaise and Berries. The Bird & Bottle Inn, Garrison, New York.

Grilled Salmon with Squaw Corn

**THE AMERICAN GRILL AT CREEKWOOD,
MICHIGAN CITY, INDIANA**

Chef Kathy de Funiak brought this recipe back from a fishing trip to northern Minnesota, where it was given to her by a Native American guide. What could be more appropriate for the menu at a restaurant called The American Grill?

6 6-ounce salmon fillets
Oil

Squaw Corn
1 tablespoon butter
1/2 cup diced red bell pepper
1/2 cup diced green bell pepper
1/2 cup diced yellow onion
3 cups fresh or frozen corn kernels
4 slices bacon, cooked, drained, and crumbled
1 teaspoon dried thyme leaves
1 cup heavy cream
Salt and freshly ground pepper to taste

1. Prepare coals for grilling.

2. To make the Squaw Corn, melt the butter in a sauté pan. Add the red and green peppers and onion and cook until just tender, about 8 minutes. Stir in the corn, bacon, and thyme.

3. Add the cream and simmer over low heat until the cream has reduced by half and the mixture has thickened. Season with salt and pepper.

4. Oil the salmon fillets on both sides and season with salt and pepper. Grill the fish for 5 minutes per side, more or less, depending on the thickness of the fillets and the desired doneness.

5. Place a bed of Squaw Corn on each plate and top with a salmon fillet.

Serves 6.

Grilled Tahini-Marinated Caribbean Red Snapper with Mango Coulis

FRIENDS LAKE INN, CHESTERTOWN, NEW YORK

Wine-tasting Dinners are held monthly at Friends Lake Inn, and a steward is always available to assist guests in ordering from the extensive wine list. Because of its fine wine cellar, the inn also holds the prestigious Best of Award of Excellence.

3/4 cup tahini paste

1/4 cup sesame oil

4 red snapper fillets, approximately 8 ounces each

2 ripe mangoes

1 tablespoon light brown sugar

1. Combine the tahini paste and oil, rub on the fillets, and allow to sit overnight, covered, in the refrigerator.

2. To make the mango coulis, peel the mangoes and cut away the meat from the pit. Place the mango meat and the brown sugar in the bowl of a food processor and purée.

3. Prepare coals for grilling.

4. Brush the excess paste from the fillets and place them on a hot grill for 1 to 2 minutes. Turn over and allow to cook until fish is cooked to medium or to the desired doneness. Remove from the grill and serve with the mango coulis.

Serves 4.

Oyster Pan Roast

DOCKSIDE GUEST QUARTERS, YORK, MAINE

Overlooking southern Maine's picturesque York Harbor, Dockside Guest Quarters offers accommodations in a variety of appropriately named buildings— the Quarterdeck, Crow's Nest, Lookout, and Captain's Quarters—in addition to the Maine House. The Restaurant at Dockside has an enthusiastic local clientèle and hosts many private parties and celebrations.

1/4 cup clam broth

1/4 cup (1/2 stick) butter

1/2 teaspoon paprika

Pinch of celery salt

2 tablespoons Worcestershire sauce

20 shucked oysters and their liquid

2 tablespoons chili sauce

1 cup heavy cream

2 slices bread, toasted

1. In the top of a double boiler over simmering water or in a heavy saucepan over low heat, place the clam broth, 2 tablespoons of the butter, the paprika, celery salt, and Worcestershire sauce. Stir gently. Add the oysters and their liquid and cook just until the edges of the oysters curl.

2. Stir in the chili sauce and heavy cream and simmer for a few more minutes.

3. Cut the toast into quarters and place four quarters in each of two warm soup plates. Pour the oyster mixture over the toast and float 1 tablespoon of the remaining butter on top of each.

Serves 2.

Gingered Snapper

MURPHIN RIDGE INN, WEST UNION, OHIO

The Dining House at Murphin Ridge Inn is overseen by a team. Innkeeper Bob Crosset rises at 4:00 every morning to prepare breakfast for overnight guests, and by mid-morning he is ready to turn over the kitchen to chef Natasha Shishkevish, who prepares lunches and dinners for inn guests as well as regular visitors from the region. Shishkevish, a graduate of the Culinary Institute of America, was teaching in Baltimore when she learned of the opening at Murphin Ridge, which provides just what she was looking for— a serene, secluded outlet for creative cooking.

8 6-ounce red snapper fillets
4 tablespoons peeled and grated fresh ginger root
2 tablespoons minced garlic
2 teaspoons chopped fresh cilantro
3 tablespoons fresh lemon juice
1 teaspoon soy sauce
3/4 cup sesame oil
All-purpose flour for dredging
2 tablespoons minced scallions, for garnish

1. Pat the fillets dry and score the skinless side three times, cutting at a diagonal just through the skin (to ensure flatness). Lay on a sheet pan, skin side down.

2. Combine the ginger root, garlic, cilantro, lemon juice, and soy sauce in a blender or mini food processor. Blend until smooth.

3. Spread the ginger mixture over the snapper fillets. Cover and chill for up to 2 hours.

4. Preheat the oven to 375 degrees F. Butter a sheet pan.

5. Heat the sesame oil to medium-high heat in a large sauté pan, using 1 1/2 tablespoons per fillet (for example, if your pan will only fit two fillets, use 3 tablespoons oil for every two fillets and sear in batches, wiping the pan out between each use).

6. Dredge the skinless side of each fillet in flour and sear this side only in the oil until golden brown and lightly crusted.

7. Carefully lift the fillets with a large spatula and lay skin side down on the prepared baking pan. Bake until just opaque, 8 to 12 minutes (do not overcook or the fish will become tough). Garnish with the scallions and serve immediately.

Serves 8.

Pan-Seared Scallops with Pancetta, Leeks, and Fresh Oregano

TURNING POINT INN, FREDERICK, MARYLAND

The gracious elegance of a bygone era is much in evidence at this lovely inn, where an Edwardian-era estate home with Georgian features is set among five acres of tree-studded lawn. There are five bedrooms in the main house, and the grounds include two guest cottages—The Carriage House and The Dairy House.

1 pound sea scallops, patted dry
2 tablespoons olive oil
1/4 pound pancetta (Italian bacon), partially cooked until fat is rendered
1 cup sliced leeks
1/4 cup dry white wine
4 tablespoons chopped fresh oregano
Salt and freshly ground pepper to taste
2 to 4 fresh oregano sprigs, for garnish

1. In a bowl, toss the scallops with 1 tablespoon of olive oil.

2. Heat a sauté pan over high heat, add the scallops, and cook until beginning to turn golden on all sides, being careful not to overcook. Transfer the scallops to a platter and keep warm until time to serve.

3. Add the pancetta and remaining olive oil to the sauté pan and sauté for 3 to 4 minutes. Add the leeks, sauté an additional 3 to 4 minutes, then add the wine and chopped oregano. Add any liquid the scallops may have exuded and reduce the mixture by half. Season with salt and pepper.

4. Divide the leek and bacon mixture between two heated plates and arrange the scallops in the center. Garnish with the oregano sprigs.

Serves 2 (or 4 as an appetizer).

Shrimp and Artichoke Romano

THE WHITE GULL INN, FISH CREEK, WISCONSIN

The White Gull warns guests not to expect whirlpools. They weren't invented when original owner Dr. Welcker founded the inn in 1896. Modern plumbing, air-conditioning, well-chosen fabrics, and fine cooking are strictly of the 1990s, however, and candlelight dinners await guests returning from excursions in the countryside. This dish is often on the dinner menu and is deceptively simple to make at home.

1/4 pound linguine

2 tablespoons clarified butter (see note page 94)

8 jumbo shrimp

6 artichoke hearts, cut in half lengthwise

2 small cloves garlic, minced

Pinch of salt

Pinch of freshly ground pepper

1/2 cup dry white wine

6 tablespoons grated Romano cheese

4 tablespoons (1/2 stick) unsalted butter, at room temperature

2 teaspoons chopped fresh parsley

1. Cook the linguine according to package instructions, until al dente. Drain well and set aside.

2. Heat the clarified butter in a sauté pan and sauté the shrimp and artichoke hearts over medium heat until the shrimp is pink but not overcooked. Add the garlic and salt and pepper and continue cooking until the garlic browns slightly, for about 20 seconds.

3. Add the wine and cheese and simmer over medium heat until the liquid is slightly thickened, for about 1 minute. Reduce the heat and add the butter, one tablespoon at a time, incorporating it into the sauce by swirling the pan. Be careful not to allow the sauce to boil (it should be the consistency of heavy cream).

4. Transfer the linguine to the pan and toss with the sauce, to distribute evenly. Divide the pasta between two plates and garnish with the parsley.

Serves 2.

Shrimp and Crabmeat Casserole

THE OLD TAVERN AT GRAFTON, GRAFTON, VERMONT

Here is a classic New England dish that has been a favorite among guests at The Old Tavern. It is easy to make and can be put together in advance, then baked at the last minute. Since the Grafton Village Cheese Factory is just up the road from the inn, the chef's choice is Grafton Classic Cheddar.

3 quarts water
1 tablespoon salt
1 tablespoon vegetable oil
1/2 pound macaroni
6 tablespoons butter
1/2 pound fresh mushrooms, sliced
1 cup light cream
1 10-ounce can condensed cream of mushroom soup
3/4 cup grated Cheddar cheese
1 pound cooked shrimp, shelled and deveined
1 cup cooked crabmeat, well picked over
1 cup soft bread crumbs
1 tablespoon butter, melted

1. Preheat the oven to 350 degrees F. Butter a 2-quart casserole.

2. Bring the water to a boil and add the salt and vegetable oil. Add the macaroni and boil rapidly for 10 minutes. Drain well and toss with 4 tablespoons of the butter.

3. Place the remaining 2 tablespoons of butter in a sauté pan and add the mushrooms. Sauté over medium heat for about 5 minutes, shaking the pan frequently.

4. Combine the cream, mushroom soup, and cheese in a small bowl and stir the mixture into the macaroni. Cut the shrimp into bite-size pieces and flake the crabmeat; add them to the macaroni, along with the mushrooms.

5. Transfer the mixture to the prepared casserole. Toss the bread crumbs with the melted butter and spread over the macaroni. Bake for 25 minutes.

Serves 6.

Crab Imperial

THE CORNER CUPBOARD INN, REHOBOTH BEACH, DELAWARE

In operation for more than fifty years, The Corner Cupboard advertises itself as "the inn that was in before inns were in." Located in a quiet residential area of a bustling resort town, it is a homey place to hole-in for weekend or longer stays, with breakfast and dinner included in the room rate from Memorial Day through mid-September. Local seafood is always on the menu.

1 pound crabmeat, carefully picked over

1/2 cup finely chopped green bell pepper

1/2 cup chopped onion

2 slices white bread, crusts removed

2 eggs, lightly beaten

Dash of Worcestershire sauce

1/8 teaspoon dry mustard

1/2 teaspoon salt

Juice of 1/2 lemon

1 tablespoon prepared mustard

Mayonnaise, as needed

Paprika

1. Preheat the oven to 400 degrees F. Butter a 1-quart casserole or individual baking shells.

2. In a large bowl combine the crabmeat, green pepper, and onion. Crumble the bread into the crabmeat mixture.

3. Add the eggs, Worcestershire, dry mustard, salt, lemon juice, prepared mustard, and enough mayonnaise to bind the mixture. Mix gently.

4. Place the crabmeat mixture in the prepared casserole or baking shells and top with a film of mayonnaise and a sprinkling of paprika. Bake until the top is lightly brown, about 20 minutes.

Serves 4.

Lobster Shiitake Crêpes

THE RED LION INN, STOCKBRIDGE, MASSACHUSETTS

The pride of western Massachusetts hostelries is a former stagecoach stop on the Albany-Boston turnpike, opened in 1773 as the Stockbridge Tavern. Today visitors enjoying the many cultural offerings of the Berkshires are certain to pause at the Red Lion—for a cool drink in a rocker on the front porch, a light meal in the Widow Bingham's Tavern, a formal lunch or dinner in the Main Dining Room, or a summer repast in the impatiens-filled courtyard.

8 tablespoons Garlic Butter

6 ounces shiitake mushrooms, sliced

8 ounces fresh cooked lobster meat

1 1/2 cups heavy cream

4 teaspoons chopped parsley

Salt and freshly ground pepper to taste

4 Crêpes (see recipe below)

Parsley sprigs

Garlic Butter

1/2 cup (1 stick) butter, at room temperature

4 teaspoons olive oil

1/2 cup minced garlic

2 tablespoons plus 2 teaspoons white wine

1 teaspoon dried oregano leaves

1 teaspoon dried basil leaves

1/8 teaspoon cayenne pepper

1. To make the Garlic Butter, combine the butter, olive oil, garlic, wine, oregano, basil, and cayenne and mix well. Chill for 1 hour.

2. Sauté the mushrooms in 8 tablespoons of the Garlic Butter until they begin to release their juices. Add the lobster meat and sauté for 1 minute.

3. Add the cream and reduce until thick, about 2 to 3 minutes. Add the chopped parsley and salt and pepper.

4. Place a warm crêpe on each of four plates. Place 1/4 cup of the lobster mixture in the center of each crêpe and roll up, using two spoons. Spoon over the remaining sauce and garnish with the parsley sprigs.

Basic Crêpes

2 eggs, at room temperature
1¼ cups milk, at room temperature
1 cup all-purpose flour
¼ teaspoon salt
¼ cup clarified butter (see note page 94)
Oil

1. Whip the eggs in a stainless steel bowl until thoroughly beaten.

2. Add the milk, flour, salt, and clarified butter and whip until smooth. Let the batter rest, covered, for 1 hour to release the air bubbles.

3. Lightly oil a well-seasoned crêpe or small omelet pan and heat it over moderate heat. Pour about ⅛ cup of the batter into the pan and quickly tilt the pan to evenly coat the bottom (the batter should be thin and even, with no holes or gaps). Cook gently for 1 to 2 minutes, until lightly browned on the edges. Turn the crêpe over and cook for 1 more minute.

4. As they are cooked, stack the crêpes on a platter and keep them warm in the oven. Or wrap the crêpes tightly in plastic wrap and refrigerate until the next day. When ready to use, warm the stacked crêpes slightly to facilitate separating.

Makes 18 to 22 crêpes.

Bouillabaisse

FOUR COLUMNS INN, NEWFANE, VERMONT

The grand Greek Revival columns gracing the façade of the 150-year-old house that is the core of Four Columns Inn were part of General Pardon Kimball's design in honor of his southern wife's childhood home. The house is one of several handsome nineteenth-century buildings surrounding the village green in one of southern Vermont's most attractive towns.

2 cups leeks, white part only, well cleaned and julienne-cut

2 cups finely chopped yellow onions

1/2 cup finely chopped fennel

1 cup olive oil

4 cups chopped seeded fresh tomatoes (use canned Italian plum
    tomatoes in winter)

5 large cloves garlic, crushed and chopped

Bouquet garni of fennel seed, bay leaf, and thyme

5 cups dry white wine

10 cups fish stock (made with haddock or cod)

4 pounds cod

2 tablespoons tomato paste

1 tablespoon saffron threads

Kosher salt and cayenne pepper to taste

1/4 cup Pernod liqueur

10 littleneck clams

20 mussels, well cleaned

2 pounds assorted whitefish

10 shrimp, shelled and deveined

1 pound cleaned and sliced calamari

Croutons made from crusty French bread

Rouille (see recipe below)

1. Slowly sauté the leeks, onion, and fennel in the olive oil until the vegetables are tender and slightly colored, about 10 minutes. Transfer to a large soup pot.

2. Add the tomatoes, garlic, bouquet garni, wine, fish stock, cod, and tomato paste. Raise the heat and cook the mixture at a rolling boil for 5 minutes, skimming as necessary. Lower the heat, add the saffron, salt, and cayenne and simmer.

3. Heat the Pernod in a separate pan, flame, and add to the soup pot. Let simmer for 20 minutes. (At this point the mixture may be held, covered and refrigerated, for several days.)

4. Bring the mixture back to the boil, add the clams, and cook for 3 minutes. Add the mussels, whitefish, and shrimp and cook for 4 minutes, or until the mussel shells open. Add the calamari and cook for 1 minute.

5. Place the fish and broth in heated bowls and serve with croutons and rouille.

Serves 10.

Rouille

5 egg yolks
1 cup vegetable oil
1/2 cup olive oil
1 teaspoon saffron threads softened in 1 tablespoon white wine
2 tablespoons minced garlic
1/2 roasted red pepper, minced (see note page 13)
Salt, white pepper, and cayenne pepper to taste
Bouillabaisse broth, as needed

1. Place the egg yolks in the bowl of a food processor and process to blend. With the motor running, gradually pour in the vegetable oil and olive oil until the mixture forms a thick paste.

2. Add the saffron (with the wine), garlic, red pepper, salt, white pepper, and cayenne and process just to blend. If the mixture is too thick, thin with liquid from the bouillabaisse.

Makes about 2 cups.

Note: Commercial mayonnaise combined with the safron, garlic, and red pepper may be used instead of the egg yolk and oil mixture.

Lobster Dublin Lawyer

DOCKSIDE GUEST QUARTERS, YORK, MAINE

Boating and boat watching are primary activities at this harborside inn and restaurant. There are whale watching and lobstering excursions, as well as harbor or York River cruises scheduled exclusively for inn guests. Maine lobster appears on the menu in many forms, including this tasty Irish rendition.

1 2-pound Maine lobster
2 tablespoons butter
1 shallot, minced
1/2 pound sea scallops
1/4 cup white wine
1/4 cup Irish whiskey
1/4 cup heavy cream
2 tablespoons garlic butter (made by combining 2 tablespoons softened
   butter with 1/2 teaspoon finely minced garlic)

1. Cook the lobster in boiling water to cover for 5 minutes. Split the lobster in half, remove the meat, and reserve the body.

2. Heat the butter in a heavy pan until frothy. Add the shallot and scallops and sauté for 2 to 3 minutes. Pour in the wine and steam briefly.

3. Add the lobster meat and heat thoroughly. Add the whiskey, let it warm, and ignite. When the flames die down, add the heavy cream and reduce but do not boil.

4. Just before serving, add the garlic butter and cook until it has melted. Place the body cavity halves on two plates, fill with the scallops and lobster, and cover with the sauce. Serve with rice or pasta.

Serves 2.

Breads and Brunch

Breads and Brunch

Italian Vegetable Frittata

Breakfast Strudel

Nonfat Egg Rellenos

Spicy Sausage Strata

Ham and Cheese Bread Pudding

Southwestern Breakfast Pie

Quiche Florentine

Sweet Georgia Vidalia Onion Pie

Spinach, Mushroom, and Arugula Tart

Cornmeal Pancakes

Orange Yogurt Pancakes

Puffed Pancake with Brandied Peach Sauce

Buckwheat Waffles

Chocolate Lovers' French Toast

Jasmine Rice Pudding

English-Style Porridge

Cherry-Stuffed French Toast

Village Inn Scones

Oatmeal Fruit Nut Scones

Sticky Buns

Lemon-Cranberry Loaf

Rosemary-Thyme Bread

Philbrook Farm Dark Bread

Raspberry Chocolate Chip Muffins

Banana Oat Muffins

Kahlua Muffins

Blueberry Morning Breakfast Cake

Almond Coffee Cake

Espresso Coffee Cake

Italian Vegetable Frittata

SEA CREST BY THE SEA, SPRING LAKE, NEW JERSEY

A Queen Anne Victorian on the Jersey Shore an hour south of New York City, Sea Crest pampers its guests with a romantic Victorian décor in the public areas and twelve individually decorated guest rooms, with names ranging from G. Washington to Casablanca. Afternoon tea and a bountiful gourmet breakfast buffet are served from the antique French sideboard in the dining room; table settings from the family collection of china, crystal, and silver enhance the experience.

2 cups sliced fresh mushrooms

1 1/2 cups chopped onion

1 1/2 cups chopped green bell pepper

2 cups chopped zucchini

1/4 cup olive oil

2 teaspoons minced garlic

10 eggs

2/3 cup light cream, half-and-half, or milk

Salt and freshly ground pepper to taste

3 cups cubed bread

4 to 8 ounces cream cheese, cut in small cubes

2 cups shredded Cheddar cheese

1. Preheat the oven to 350 degrees F. Grease a 9 x 13-inch casserole.

2. Combine the vegetables and sauté in the oil in batches (or use two frying pans) over medium-high heat until they take on a golden color. Add the garlic for the last few minutes, to prevent it from becoming too brown.

3. In a large bowl, beat the eggs with the cream until they are well combined. Add the sautéed vegetables, the salt and pepper, cubed bread, cream cheese, and Cheddar cheese. Mix until combined and pour into the prepared pan. Bake for about 1 hour, until golden brown on top and cooked through. Cut in squares to serve.

Serves 6 to 8.

Note: This dish can be prepared the night before and refrigerated overnight, covered, before baking.

Breakfast Strudel

ASA RANSOM HOUSE, CLARENCE, NEW YORK

*The gourmet cuisine at Asa Ransom House has been featured in **Bon Appétit** and **Gourmet** magazines, and this strudel is one of the most popular breakfast entrées. Innkeeper Judy Lenz, who owns the inn with her husband, Robert, created the dish as a way of combining all the basic elements of a classic breakfast, but with a unique presentation.*

8 eggs
1/2 cup milk
1/2 cup sour cream
1/4 cup finely chopped red bell pepper
1 scallion, minced, or 1 tablespoon chopped chives
1 tablespoon butter or vegetable spray
1 sheet frozen puff pastry, thawed
1/3 pound thinly sliced ham or corned beef
4 thin slices Lorraine Swiss cheese
1 egg and 2 tablespoons water for egg wash

1. Preheat the oven to 375 degrees F. Line a baking sheet with parchment paper.

2. Combine the eggs, milk, and sour cream.

3. Sauté the red pepper and scallion in a frying pan with the butter or vegetable spray. Add the egg mixture and scramble loosely over low heat; set aside.

4. Roll out the sheet of pastry into a 12 x 17-inch rectangle. Place the ham or corned beef on top of the pastry. Lengthwise, down the center third, evenly mound the scrambled eggs. Place the cheese slices evenly on top of the eggs.

5. Combine the ingredients for the egg wash, beating lightly, and brush all of the edges of the pastry with the wash. Fold one third of the pastry and meat over the eggs and then the last third over the top. Seal the edges well and brush the top of the strudel with egg wash.

6. Transfer the strudel to the prepared baking sheet and bake for about 30 minutes, until the top is nicely browned.

Serves 4 to 6.

Nonfat Egg Rellenos

THE GREY WHALE INN, FORT BRAGG, CALIFORNIA

The Mendocino coast of northern California is known for its scenery and out-door activities—beaches, hiking trails, whale watching—and to contribute to the wholesome environment, innkeeper Colette Bailey has created a fat-free, cholesterol-free brunch entrée.

3 green bell peppers

3 red bell peppers

3/4 pound nonfat Cheddar cheese, grated

3/4 pound nonfat Monterey Jack or mozzarella cheese, grated

2 cups nonfat cottage cheese

1 teaspoon seasoned salt

1/2 teaspoon white pepper

2 tablespoons all-purpose flour

2 cups nonfat sour cream

2 1/4 cups egg substitute

2 cups salsa, preferably freshly homemade

1. Preheat the oven to 350 degrees F. Grease a 10 1/2 x 14 3/4 x 2 1/3-inch casserole.

2. Seed the peppers and slice lengthwise into 1/4-inch pieces. Layer the pepper slices and the cheese in the casserole until all are used.

3. Process the cottage cheese in a food processor until smooth. Add the seasoned salt, pepper, flour, and sour cream and process for 5 seconds more.

4. Place the cottage cheese mixture in a large bowl. Add the egg substitute and beat until well blended. Pour over the pepper and cheese mixture.

5. Bake for 1 hour, until puffed and golden and set in the center. Remove from the oven and let stand for 10 minutes before serving. Place the salsa in a separate bowl and serve.

Serves 16 to 18.

Spicy Sausage Strata

WICKWOOD INN, SAUGATUCK, MICHIGAN

One of Julee Rosso Miller's secret ingredients in this recipe is Low-Fat Blend, which she whips up at the beginning of every week and keeps on hand to use by the cup or spoonful in myriad ways. It can replace sour cream, mayonnaise, or heavy cream in mousses, sauces, muffins, and dips. The blending must be done by hand or with a blender; the food processor tends to break down the mixture and make it watery instead of creamy.

6 slices white bread, crusts removed and saved

5 eggs

3 egg whites

1 tablespoon dry mustard

2 cups skim milk

1 cup Low-Fat Blend (see recipe below)

1 cup heavy cream

Dash of Tabasco sauce

1 pound zesty hot sausage of your choice, cooked and drained well

1/2 tablespoon finely chopped fresh sage

2 cups stemmed and quartered fresh mushrooms, sautéed in a small
    amount of butter

4 1/2 ounces Brie cheese, including rind

1/2 cup chopped scallions

Freshly ground pepper to taste

1/2 cup Parmesan shards (see note below)

1. Spray a 13 x 9-inch pan with olive oil spray.

2. Spread the reserved bread crusts over the bottom of the pan and arrange the whole slices of bread on top.

3. Place the eggs, egg whites, mustard, milk, Low-Fat Blend, heavy cream, and Tabasco in a bowl and blend well. Pour this mixture over the bread, cover the pan, and refrigerate overnight.

4. The next morning, preheat the oven to 350 degrees F.

5. Sprinkle over the top of the egg and bread mixture the sausage, sage, and mushrooms and dot with small pieces of the Brie. (Lift the bread and tuck some of the toppings underneath to avoid having them all rise to the top during baking.) Sprinkle on the scallions, season with pepper, and top with the Parmesan shards.

6. Bake for 45 minutes, or until golden.

Serves 8.

Note: Parmesan shards are made by using a vegetable peeler to shave curls of cheese from a block of Parmesan.

Low-Fat Blend

1 cup nonfat plain yogurt
1 cup nonfat cottage cheese

Place the ingredients in a blender (not a food processor) and blend until smooth, or blend by hand.

Makes 2 cups.

Ham and Cheese Bread Pudding

VINTNERS INN, SANTA ROSA, CALIFORNIA

As the name suggests, this inn is both adjacent to a vineyard and located at the exact crossroads of the Sonoma County wine country. The forty-five guest rooms are decorated in the French country style, and amenities abound— including spa facilities and a nationally acclaimed restaurant.

4 eggs

6 egg yolks

1 quart light cream

1 quart half-and-half

2 1/2 cups grated Cheddar cheese

2 1/2 cups grated smoked Gouda cheese

1 small onion, diced

4 cups ground smoked ham

1/4 cup Dijon mustard

1/3 cup sugar

2 tablespoons minced fresh oregano, or 1 tablespoon dried

1 loaf brioche bread, crusts removed, cubed

1. Preheat the oven to 375 degrees F. Grease a 13 x 9-inch baking pan. Have on hand a larger pan in which the first pan can sit while baking.

2. Beat the eggs, egg yolks, cream, and half-and-half in a large bowl. Add the remaining ingredients, except the bread cubes, and mix well. Add the bread cubes and let soak for 1 hour.

3. Pour the mixture into the prepared pan. Place the pan in a larger pan, fill the larger pan with water to reach three-quarters of the way up the sides of the smaller pan, and bake for 35 to 40 minutes, or until the center is firm.

Serves 8 to 10.

Note: The pudding also may be made in individual ramekins, in which case the cooking time should be 20 to 25 minutes.

Southwestern Breakfast Pie

THE CAPTAIN'S HOUSE INN, CHATHAM, MASSACHUSETTS

This is about as far away from home as southwestern fare gets. At the Captain's House, the individual pies are accompanied with a dollop of salsa and a wedge of melon.

1 large onion, chopped
1 cup chopped red bell pepper
1 cup chopped green bell pepper
Oil for sautéing
8 eggs plus 3 eggs
1 pound bacon, fried crisp and broken into bite-size pieces
2 cups coarsely grated Monterey Jack pepper cheese
1 1-pound bag frozen hash brown potatoes, thawed
1/4 cup half-and-half

1. Spray 12 extra-large muffin cups with vegetable spray.

2. Sauté the onion and peppers in a small amount of olive or vegetable oil and let cool.

3. In a large bowl whisk the 8 eggs until foamy. Add the onion and pepper mixture, bacon, cheese, and hash browns and combine well.

4. Fill each of the muffin cups three-fourths full. Cover the tin with foil and refrigerate overnight or continue with the recipe.

5. Preheat the oven to 350 degrees F.

6. Whisk together the 3 eggs and the half-and-half. Before baking, distribute the mixture evenly over the top of each muffin cup. Bake for 45 minutes.

Serves 12.

Note: If you cannot locate Pepper Jack cheese, use plain Monterey Jack and add 1/4 cup chopped jalapeño peppers.

Quiche Florentine

HARBOR HOUSE, ELK, CALIFORNIA

Situated on a bluff overlooking Greenwood Landing, once a busy port for lumber schooners plying the Mendocino coast, the main building at Harbor Inn was built in 1916 as an executive residence for the Goodyear Redwood Lumber Company. The ambience of a leisurely, romantic era is maintained today, and since the inn operates on a modified American plan (including dinner and breakfast), good food is key to the overall experience.

1/3 cup minced onion
2 tablespoons butter
1/2 cup cooked and drained spinach
1/4 cup milk
Freshly ground black pepper
Freshly grated nutmeg
4 eggs
1 1/2 cups cottage cheese
1/2 cup freshly grated Parmesan cheese
1 unbaked pastry shell
Tomato slices (optional)
Melted butter

1. Preheat the oven to 375 degrees F.

2. In a frying pan, sauté the onion in the butter over medium heat until soft but not browned. Add the spinach and sauté, stirring, for 2 minutes.

3. Remove the frying pan from the heat and add the milk, pepper, and nutmeg. Let cool slightly.

4. Combine the eggs, cottage cheese, and Parmesan cheese, using an electric mixer until almost smooth (leave some texture). Add the spinach mixture, combine well, and pour into the pastry shell. Arrange tomato slices on top of the custard mixture if you wish.

5. Drizzle a small amount of melted butter over the top and bake for 35 minutes. Allow to stand for a few minutes before cutting into wedges and serving.

Serves 6.

Sweet Georgia Vidalia Onion Pie

THE WATERFORD INNE, WATERFORD, MAINE

Sherry and Mike Justiss of Savannah, Georgia, have long been guests of the Waterford Inne, and each spring when Vidalia onions are in season, they send the inn a ten-pound box. This recipe, now a favorite with guests, was included in the package one year. It must be made with Vidalias; other onions are too watery.

3 to 4 slices bacon

3 tablespoons butter or margarine

3 cups thinly sliced Vidalia onions

1 9-inch deep-dish pie shell, baked

1/2 cup milk

1 1/2 cups sour cream

1 teaspoon salt

2 eggs, lightly beaten

3 tablespoons all-purpose flour

1/4 to 1/2 cup grated Cheddar cheese

1. Preheat the oven to 325 degrees F.

2. Fry the bacon in a large frying pan until crisp. Remove from the pan, drain on paper towels, and crumble. Set aside.

3. Add the butter to the bacon pan with the bacon grease and heat until melted. Add the onions and sauté over medium heat until lightly brown. Spoon the onions into the baked pie shell.

4. Combine the milk, sour cream, salt, eggs, and flour in a bowl and mix well. Add about two-thirds of the grated Cheddar. Pour the mixture over the onions.

5. Scatter the crumbled bacon and the remaining cheese over the top and bake for 30 minutes or until the center is firm.

Serves 8.

Spinach, Mushroom, and Arugula Tart

PILGRIM'S INN, DEER ISLE, MAINE

At Pilgrim's Inn the enticements of the out-of-doors, where gardens and lawns lead to the water's edge, vie with the warmth of the colonial interiors. Guests enjoy fancy hors d'oeuvres and cocktails in the Common Room against a back-drop of an eight-foot-wide fireplace and beehive oven. The barn, complete with hand-hewn beams and antique farm tools, houses the dining room.

1¼ cups all-purpose flour

⅛ teaspoon salt

6 tablespoons cold butter

4 tablespoons water

10 ounces spinach, washed and stems removed

1 onion, minced

1 clove garlic, minced

1 cup chopped fresh mushrooms

2 tablespoons pine nuts, toasted

3 tablespoons butter

1 cup chopped arugula

Pinch of freshly ground pepper

Pinch of cayenne pepper

3 ounces cream cheese, at room temperature

⅔ cup sour cream

3 eggs

⅓ cup freshly grated Parmesan cheese

1. Preheat the oven to 400 degrees F.

2. Place the flour and salt in a mixing bowl and stir together. Cut the 6 tablespoons butter in pieces and cut into the flour with a pastry blender or two table knives, until the mixture resembles small peas.

3. Sprinkle 1 tablespoon of the water over part of the mixture, gently toss with a fork, and push to one side of the bowl. Repeat with the remaining 3 tablespoons water until the entire mixture is moistened. Form the dough into a ball.

4. Roll out the dough to a 13-inch circle on a lightly floured surface. Transfer to an 11-inch tart pan, trim the pastry even with the edge of the pan. Partially bake the crust for 15 minutes.

5. Place the spinach in a sauté pan and cook over medium heat only until wilted, using the water that sticks to the leaves. Drain and squeeze out excess liquid. Finely chop the spinach and set aside.

6. In a large sauté pan, cook the onion, garlic, mushrooms, and pine nuts in the 3 tablespoons butter over low heat until the onion is tender but not brown. Stir in the spinach, arugula, and black and red pepper and set aside.

7. In the bowl of an electric mixer, beat the cream cheese and sour cream until smooth. Add the eggs and beat on low speed until just combined. Stir in the spinach mixture and the Parmesan cheese.

8. Pour the filling into the prebaked tart shell, and bake for 20 to 25 minutes, or until a knife inserted near the center comes out clean.

Serves 8 to 10.

Cornmeal Pancakes

WILDFLOWER INN, JACKSON, WYOMING

Ken and Sherrie Jern and their daughter, Jessica, began constructing their house and bed and breakfast inn in 1988. Using local methods and materials, they hoped to give a feeling of what it's like to stay in a log home. Their guests are fascinated with the structure and come to breakfast full of questions about how the logs are put together.

2 cups yellow cornmeal
1 cup all-purpose flour
1 tablespoon sugar
1 teaspoon salt
1 teaspoon baking soda
1 teaspoon baking powder
2 cups buttermilk or plain yogurt
1/2 cup milk
1/4 cup vegetable oil
2 eggs
1 to 2 cups blueberries (optional)

1. Combine the dry ingredients in a large bowl and mix well.

2. Add the buttermilk, milk, oil, and eggs and stir until all ingredients are incorporated. Gently stir in the blueberries if you are using them. Let sit for 5 to 10 minutes.

3. Heat a griddle or large frying pan to medium hot and oil lightly. Use a 1/4-cup measuring cup to ladle the batter onto the griddle. Cook until bubbles form on the surface; turn to brown the second side.

Serves 8.

Orange Yogurt Pancakes

BEAVER POND FARM INN, WARREN, VERMONT

In ski country, hearty breakfasts are the norm, and Betty Hansen's are among the best. A stay at Beaver Pond Farm includes not only bountiful breakfasts but prix-fixe dinners three nights a week and après-ski snacks. As one satisfied guest has remarked, "At last, a family ski trip with dignity."

2 cups all-purpose flour
2/3 cup sugar
2 teaspoons baking soda
1 teaspoon baking powder
2 eggs, lightly beaten
1 1/2 cups plain yogurt
2/3 cup orange juice
Orange slices, strawberries, and yogurt, for garnish

1. In a large bowl, combine the flour, sugar, baking soda, and baking powder and mix well.

2. Combine the eggs, yogurt, and orange juice in a separate bowl.

3. Pour the wet ingredients into the dry ingredients and stir just to combine.

4. Make the pancakes on a lightly greased hot griddle. Serve immediately, garnished with orange slices or strawberries and a dollop of yogurt.

Serves 4.

Puffed Pancake with Brandied Peach Sauce

COWSLIP'S BELLE BED AND BRAKFAST, ASHLAND, OREGON

Cowslip's Belle is an award-winning bed and brakfast, and its owner/chef, Jon Reinhardt, is part of the reason. His biscotti and chocolate-dipped macaroons have been marketed to local and regional merchants, and truffles made by his wife, Carmen, appear on each guest's pillow at night. After a good night's sleep, guests gather in the dining room for a scrumptious breakfast, "with a hearty serving of lively conversation."

Pancake

6 eggs

1 teaspoon pure vanilla extract

3 teaspoons sugar

1 cup all-purpose flour

1²/₃ cups milk

2 tablespoons melted butter

Brandied Peach Sauce

1/4 cup unsalted butter

4 cups sliced fresh peaches, or frozen

1 cup sugar

3 or 4 tablespoons brandy

1. Preheat the oven to 450 degrees F. Spray four individual gratin dishes with vegetable cooking spray, covering inside surfaces completely.

2. To make the pancake, in a blender combine the eggs, vanilla, and sugar. Add the flour 1/2 cup at a time and blend. Add the milk and blend, making sure the flour is completely incorporated. Add the melted butter and blend.

3. Pour the batter into the prepared baking dishes. Bake until puffed and browned around the edges, about 20 minutes.

4. To make the sauce (while pancakes are baking), melt the butter in a large frying pan, add the peaches, and sauté until cooked through, about 5 minutes. Add the sugar and cook, stirring, until the liquid is no longer grainy and has thickened. Add the brandy and stir.

5. To serve, spoon the hot sauce onto the hot pancakes. The sauce will sizzle as the dishes are taken to the table.

Serves 4.

Buckwheat Waffles

WILDFLOWER INN, JACKSON, WYOMING

Innkeeper/breakfast chef Sherrie Jern promises that these wonderfully light waffles never stick to the iron. At Wildflower Inn, they are served with fresh strawberries and warm maple syrup.

1½ cups buckwheat flour
1½ cups all-purpose flour
4 teaspoons baking powder
1½ teaspoons baking soda
1 teaspoon salt
4 tablespoons sugar
6 eggs
3 cups buttermilk
1 cup (2 sticks) butter, melted and cooled

1. Preheat a waffle iron.

2. Combine the dry ingredients in a large bowl.

3. Beat the eggs, buttermilk, and melted butter together in a separate bowl, until well combined. Add to the dry ingredients and stir until just blended.

4. Ladle the batter into the heated waffle iron and cook until the waffles stop steaming and are brown and crisp.

Serves 10.

Chocolate Lovers' French Toast

THE INN AT HARBOR HEAD, KENNEBUNKPORT, MAINE

Joan Sutter and her husband, Dave, have created a special romantic hideaway overlooking Cape Porpoise Harbor and the ocean. One of the best views in the house is from the elegant dining room filled with crystal and pewter and enhanced by original stenciling, where classical music accompanies an extensive gourmet breakfast. French toast in various renditions is a specialty; this one is truly a chocoholic's fantasy.

Raspberry Sauce

1 10-ounce package frozen raspberries

1/2 cup sugar

1 tablespoon fresh lemon juice

2 tablespoons Chambord liqueur

Toast

3/4 cup sweet ground chocolate (Ghirardelli),

   or 3/4 cup Dutch process cocoa combined with 3/4 cup sugar

1/2 cup boiling water

6 eggs

1 cup light cream

24 slices Vienna-style white bread

Melted butter, for sautéing

Garnish

1 pint fresh raspberries

Whipped cream

2 tablespoons semisweet chocolate shavings

16 fresh mint leaves

Confectioners' sugar

1. To make the sauce (this can be done ahead), heat the frozen raspberries, sugar, and lemon juice to boiling over medium heat, and cook for 5 minutes. Remove from heat, purée in a food processor or blender, and push through a sieve to strain out the seeds. Add the liqueur. Reheat before serving.

2. To make the toast, blend the chocolate or cocoa and boiling water in a food processor and let cool slightly. Add the eggs and cream and blend well.

3. Pour the chocolate mixture into a large bowl and dip the bread slices in the mixture to coat. Set aside until all are coated.

4. Heat a griddle, brush it with melted butter, and cook the dipped slices, turning to cook evenly, about 2 minutes per side.

5. To serve, place a heaping spoonful of sauce on each plate. Overlap the bread slices on top of the sauce (to resemble flower petals) and top with fresh raspberries and a rosette of whipped cream topped with chocolate curls. Garnish the plate with mint leaves, drizzle the remaining sauce over the top of the toast, and sprinkle lightly with confectioners' sugar.

Serves 8.

Jasmine Rice Pudding

THE GREY WHALE INN, FORT BRAGG, CALIFORNIA

Jasmine rice is a fragrant long-grain rice imported from Thailand, increasingly available at supermarkets or specialty foods stores. Innkeeper Colette Bailey combines it with low-fat ingredients to make a breakfast pudding for the most health-conscious of her guests.

1 cup Jasmine rice
2 cups water
1 cup golden raisins
1 1/2 cups sugar
2 tablespoons cornstarch
2 teaspoons ground cinnamon
1/4 teaspoon salt
1 cup egg substitute
5 cups skim milk
2 tablespoons fresh lemon juice

1. Stir together the rice and water in a 6-quart saucepan. Heat to boiling, stirring once or twice, then reduce the heat, cover, and simmer for 18 minutes without removing the cover.

2. Preheat the oven to 350 degrees F. Butter a 3-quart casserole and set out a larger pan to hold a hot water bath.

3. Place the raisins in a small bowl, cover with hot water, and allow to plump for several minutes. Drain well.

4. In a 1-quart bowl, stir together the sugar, cornstarch, cinnamon, and salt. Add the egg substitute and 1 cup of the milk and stir to blend well.

5. Add the drained raisins and the lemon juice to the rice and combine well. Stir in 2 cups of the milk and then the sugar-egg mixture. Add the final 2 cups of milk and stir well.

6. Carefully pour the mixture into the prepared casserole. Place the casserole in the larger pan and fill the pan with hot water, to come halfway up the sides of the casserole. Bake for 1 1/2 hours, stirring occasionally. The finished pudding will be creamy but not set.

7. Set the pudding aside for about 1/2 hour before serving, stirring a couple of times to assure that the rice and raisins are distributed throughout the pudding.

Serves 12 to 16.

English-Style Porridge

THE CAPTAIN LORD MANSION, KENNEBUNKPORT, MAINE

The name of this inn says it all—a large and lovely sea captain's house on the coast of Maine, carefully decorated with touches of period antiques by innkeepers Bev Davis and her husband, Rick Litchfield. Refugees from the corporate world of advertising, they searched New England until they found the perfect spot for a complete change of lifestyle.

4 cups water
1 teaspoon salt
2 cups quick-cooking oatmeal
5 tablespoons butter
1/4 teaspoon cinnamon
1/4 teaspoon ground nutmeg
2 heaping tablespoons light brown sugar
2 ounces maple syrup
2/3 can (12-ounce) evaporated milk

1. Bring the water and salt to a boil in a large saucepan. Add the oatmeal and cook for 1 minute, stirring constantly.

2. Remove from the heat and stir in the remaining ingredients. Serve immediately.

Serves 6.

Cherry-Stuffed French Toast

THE WHITE GULL INN, FISH CREEK, WISCONSIN

The Door Peninsula in northern Wisconsin has miles of apple and cherry orchards, so Cherry-Stuffed French Toast is a natural for this turn-of-the-century inn situated in a charming coastal village. An unusual feature of life at the White Gull Inn is the fact that hearty breakfasts are served until noon.

1 loaf egg bread, unsliced
1 8-ounce package cream cheese, at room temperature
1/3 cup heavy cream
1 cup pitted tart red cherries, drained
Oil for griddle
6 eggs, well beaten
Cinnamon
Confectioners' sugar

1. Slice the bread into 1 1/2-inch slices. Cut each slice lengthwise three-quarters of the way down, so that you have almost formed two slices of bread (the 1/4 inch at the bottom will hold the entire piece together). Set aside.

2. Using an electric mixer at medium speed, combine the cream cheese, heavy cream, and cherries.

3. Spread approximately 1/4 cup of the mixture into the pocket of each slice of bread. Gently press the two sides together, distributing the filling evenly.

4. Lightly oil a griddle and heat until hot but not smoking. Dip each slice of the stuffed bread into the beaten egg to coat all sides. Place the bread on the griddle, sprinkle with cinnamon, and turn when golden brown; continue cooking until the second side is brown.

5. Remove the cooked slices to a cutting board and gently slice each piece in half diagonally. Garnish with confectioners' sugar. Arrange the triangles on warmed individual serving plates and serve immediately with hot maple syrup.

Serves 4.

Note: The filling can be prepared in advance, with your choice of fruits.

Village Inn Scones

THE VILLAGE INN, LENOX, MASSACHUSETTS

This recipe was given to innkeepers Cliff Rudisill and Ray Wilson by John Tovey, owner and chef at Miller Howe Country House Hotel at Windermere in the Lake District, when they complimented him on making the best scones in all of England. They are regularly served at the high teas following the Village Inn's annual series of chamber concerts. The yield is substantial (the recipe even can be doubled successfully), but the dough freezes well before baking.

4 cups flour

1/2 teaspoon baking soda

1/2 teaspoon salt

1 1/2 teaspoons baking powder

1 cup (2 sticks) butter, at room temperature, cut into small cubes

3 1/2 tablespoons sugar

5 eggs, lightly beaten

1/2 cup milk (more or less)

1. Preheat the oven to 425 degrees F.

2. Combine the flour, baking soda, salt, and baking powder and sift into a large bowl.

3. Drop the cubes of butter into the flour mixture and blend gently with the fingers until the mixture resembles coarse cornmeal.

4. Sprinkle the sugar over the mixture and add the eggs. Mix gently with the hands until well combined (do not overwork). Continuing to use the hands, blend in enough milk to make a soft but not sticky dough.

5. Pat the dough onto a floured surface to form a square 1 inch thick. Cut the dough into small triangles (the base of each should be about 2 inches long). Bake on an ungreased baking sheet for 18 minutes.

Makes about 3 dozen scones.

Note: For browner scones, brush the tops with lightly beaten egg white before baking.

Oatmeal Fruit Nut Scones

THE LODGE AT LAKE CLEAR, LAKE CLEAR, NEW YORK

This is one of owner/chef Cathy Hohmeyer's own concoctions, and it is a recipe frequently requested by guests. The scones are simple to make at the last minute and are best served hot from the oven. Alas, they do not keep well.

1/2 cup milk

2 eggs, lightly beaten

2 to 4 tablespoons sugar

1/2 teaspoon pure vanilla extract

1/2 teaspoon salt

1/4 cup (1/2 stick) butter, melted

1 3/4 cups all-purpose flour

2 teaspoons baking powder

1/2 cup rolled oats

1/2 cup your choice (in any combination) raspberries, blueberries,
   chopped walnuts, chopped dates, raisins

Dash of ground cinnamon

1. Preheat the oven to 350 degrees F.

2. In a large bowl, combine the milk, eggs, sugar, vanilla, salt, and butter. Add the flour, baking powder, and rolled oats. Mix just until blended.

3. Add your own combination of fruits and nuts and a dash of cinnamon.

4. Spoon onto an ungreased baking sheet, as for a large cookie. Bake for about 15 minutes—less if you like them soft, more if you like a crunchy outside.

Serves 6 or 8.

Sticky Buns

THE CAPTAIN LORD MANSION, KENNEBUNKPORT, MAINE

Convenience foods sometimes have their day, as this recipe makes amply clear.

1 loaf frozen bread dough, thawed
1/4 cup chopped nuts
2 tablespoons raisins
1/2 cup butterscotch pudding mix (not instant)
1 teaspoon ground cinnamon
1/2 cup sugar
6 tablespoons (3/4 stick) butter
1 tablespoon light brown sugar

1. Thoroughly grease the bottom of a tube pan.

2. Slice the bread dough in half lengthwise, then cut each half into 6 pieces.

3. Sprinkle the nuts and raisins over the bottom of the prepared pan. Place the bread pieces over the nuts and raisins.

4. Blend together the pudding mix and cinnamon and sprinkle over the bread pieces.

5. Place the sugar, butter, and brown sugar in a small saucepan and bring to a boil, stirring, over medium heat. Remove from the heat, cool to warm, and pour over the bread pieces. Cover the pan with a cloth and let rise overnight in the refrigerator.

6. Preheat the oven to 350 degrees F. Bake the buns for 30 minutes. Let stand for 2 to 3 minutes, then turn upside down onto a plate and serve.

Makes 12.

Lemon-Cranberry Loaf

THE WAUWINET, NANTUCKET, MASSACHUSETTS

Two ship captains built the Wauwinet House in 1876 on a spit of land eight miles from the center of town, bordered by Nantucket Bay on one side and the Atlantic on the other. Popular for its shore dinners, the restaurant soon added lodging and quickly became a social center of the island. In the late 1980s, the historic hotel was renovated by Stephen and Jill Karp, longtime Nantucket vacationers, and its casual elegance in a matchless location now makes it a very special destination. The inn's Topper's restaurant, overseen by chef Peter Wallace, is known for its innovative country inn cuisine, with local lobster, crab, scallops, steamers, striped bass, bushberries, and cranberries regularly featured.

1 cup (2 sticks) butter, at room temperature

2 cups sugar

3 eggs, at room temperature

3 tablespoons fresh lemon juice

Finely grated rind of 3 lemons

3 cups sifted all-purpose flour

1/2 teaspoon baking soda

1/2 teaspoon salt

1 cup buttermilk

2 cups chopped cranberries

Glaze

1/2 cup lemon juice

1/3 cup sugar

1. Preheat the oven to 350 degrees F. Grease eight mini loaf pans (2 x 3 inches) or one 9-inch bundt pan (if using a bundt or tube pan, grease and dust with flour).

2. In the bowl of an electric mixer, cream the butter until light. Add the sugar and beat well, scraping down the sides and bottom of the bowl.

3. Add the eggs, one at a time, mixing well and scraping after each addition. Add the lemon juice and rind.

4. Sift the dry ingredients into a separate bowl. Add the dry ingredients to the butter mixture in thirds, alternately with the buttermilk, and beat only to combine.

5. Using a plastic spatula, fold in the cranberries.

6. Turn the batter into the prepared pans and bake for 20 to 30 minutes for mini loaves and at least 1 hour for a bundt pan, until a toothpick inserted in the center comes out clean.

7. While the loaves are baking, prepare the glaze. In a stainless steel pan, cook the lemon juice and sugar over low to medium heat just until the sugar dissolves, stirring constantly (do not boil).

8. Brush the glaze over the loaves or cake as they cool in the pan.

Makes 8 mini loaves or 1 9-inch cake.

Rosemary-Thyme Bread

STE. ANNE'S COUNTRY INN AND SPA, GRAFTON, ONTARIO

The stone turrets, archways, and garden walls of the sprawling complex that is Ste. Anne's Country Inn give a medieval feel to this peaceful retreat situated among the rolling hills of southern Ontario. Originally a farm called Sunnyside, the property was bought by a Texas family as a summer home in 1939, renamed Ste. Anne's, and given the somewhat monastic look it has today. Far from being a monastery, Ste. Anne's pampers its guests with comfortable and attractive rooms, spa facilities, and wonderfully wholesome food. Vegetables and herbs come from the inn's organic garden.

1 1/4 cups warm water (110 degrees F)

2 tablespoons sugar

1 package active dry yeast

2 cups plus 1 cup all-purpose flour

1 cup whole wheat flour

1 teaspoon salt

1 tablespoon dried rosemary leaves

1 1/2 tablespoons dried thyme leaves

1. Place the water and sugar in the bowl of an electric mixer. Add the yeast and allow to sit until foamy.

2. Add the 2 cups all-purpose flour, the whole wheat flour, salt, and herbs. Mix well on low speed. If the dough is too moist, add enough of the 1 cup flour until the dough pulls away cleanly from the sides of the bowl.

3. Using a kneading hook, or by hand on a floured surface, knead the dough for about 5 minutes. Place in a greased bowl, cover, and allow to rise.

4. When the dough has doubled in bulk, punch down and place on a floured surface. Knead lightly and shape into a cylinder. Place on a greased cookie sheet, slit the top in several places, and allow to rise until almost double in bulk.

5. Preheat the oven to 400 degrees F.

6. Bake the loaf for about 30 minutes, until it sounds hollow when tapped.

   Makes 1 loaf.

Note: This recipe can be varied easily. For twelve-grain bread, use 2 cups whole wheat flour, 1/2 cup all-purpose flour, and 3/4 cup twelve-grain mixture. For rye bread, use 1 cup each of all-purpose, whole wheat, and rye flour. The variations can be made with or without the herbs.

Philbrook Farm Dark Bread

PHILBROOK FARM INN, SHELBURNE, NEW HAMPSHIRE

Philbrook Farm Inn took in its first guests in 1853 and is currently being operated by the fourth and fifth generations of the same family. Dinner and breakfast are provided for guests, with home-style New England cooking the order of the day. None of today's Philbrooks knows the origin of this favorite bread recipe. "It has been in our family for several generations."

1 1/2 cups graham flour
2 cups all-purpose flour
1/2 cup light brown sugar
1/2 cup molasses
2 cups sour milk or buttermilk
2 teaspoons baking soda
1 teaspoon salt

1. Preheat the oven to 350 degrees F. Grease a 9 x 4 1/2-inch loaf pan.

2. Combine all the ingredients in a large bowl and mix well. Place in the prepared pan and bake for about 1 hour, until a tester inserted in the center comes out clean.

   Makes 1 loaf.

Raspberry Chocolate Chip Muffins

SEA CREST BY THE SEA, SPRING LAKE, NEW JERSEY

Carol and John Kirby welcome guests at every season and make the most of outdoor life in their beachside location. A fleet of bikes is available, and a favorite summertime activity is croquet on the lawn. Also available in summer are John's fresh-picked raspberries, used in this favorite muffin recipe. But as Carol says, "They are fabulous any time. In winter, frozen raspberries work well too. For a nice touch, dust with powdered sugar before serving."

2 cups all-purpose flour
1/4 to 1/2 cup sugar
1 1/2 teaspoons baking powder
1/2 teaspoon salt
1/4 teaspoon ground nutmeg
1/2 cup butter, melted and cooled
1 egg, lightly beaten
1 cup raspberries
1/4 cup mini chocolate chips

1. Preheat the oven to 400 degrees F. Grease cups of a muffin tin.

2. In a large bowl, stir together the flour, sugar, baking powder, salt, and nutmeg. In a small bowl or measuring cup, combine the butter and egg.

3. Make a well in the center of the dry ingredients, add the butter mixed with the egg, and stir until just combined (do not beat). Gently stir in the berries and chocolate chips.

4. Bake for 15 to 20 minutes, until the tops are golden and a cake tester comes out clean. Cool in the pan for 5 minutes, then remove the muffins and serve. Or place on a wire rack to continue cooling.

Makes 12 muffins.

Banana Oat Muffins

ANGEL OF THE SEA BED AND BREAKFAST,
CAPE MAY, NEW JERSEY

Consistently listed as one of the top ten bed and breakfast inns in the United States, Angel of the Sea is the result of one of the most major restorations of a Victorian structure ever undertaken in New Jersey. The mansion was built in 1850 for chemist William Weightman of Philadelphia and withstood a move in two sections to its present ocean-view location in 1881. After subsequent years as an inn, boarding house, and ultimately a derelict structure, "The Angel" opened for business in 1989.

1 1/2 cups oat bran

1/2 cup sugar

1 cup all-purpose flour

1 tablespoon baking powder

1 teaspoon nonfat dry milk

1/2 cup chopped walnuts

2 egg whites

1 cup skim milk

1/4 cup corn oil

1 tablespoon fresh lemon juice

1 teaspoon pure vanilla extract

2 ripe bananas, mashed

1/2 teaspoon salt

1/2 cup chopped walnuts

1. Preheat the oven to 400 degrees F. Grease and flour the cups of a muffin tin.

2. In a large bowl, combine the dry ingredients, including the walnuts.

3. In a separate bowl, beat the egg whites until stiff but not dry, then mix in the remaining ingredients.

4. Add the wet ingredients to the dry ingredients and mix only until moistened. The batter will be lumpy. Spoon the batter into the prepared muffin tins and bake for 15 to 20 minutes, until the tops are brown.

Makes 1 dozen.

Kahlua Muffins

LA CORSETTE MAISON INN, NEWTON, IOWA

To spend the night at La Corsette Maison is to be the personal houseguest of Kay Owen. Her opulent mission-style mansion was built in 1909, and the oak woodwork, art nouveau stained glass windows, brass lighting fixtures, and even some of the original furnishings remain.

1³/4 cups all-purpose flour

2¹/2 teaspoons baking powder

2 tablespoons sugar

³/4 teaspoon salt

1 egg, well beaten

¹/2 cup milk

¹/4 cup Kahlua liqueur

¹/3 cup melted butter or salad oil

¹/3 cup chopped walnuts

1. Preheat the oven to 400 degrees F. Grease cups of a muffin tin.

2. Sift the dry ingredients into a large bowl.

3. Combine the egg, milk, Kahlua, and butter.

4. Make a well in the center of the dry ingredients and pour in the egg mixture. Stir just until the dry ingredients are moistened. Stir in the nuts.

5. Drop the batter by tablespoon into the prepared pan, filling each cup two-thirds full. Bake for 12 minutes.

Makes 12 muffins.

Blueberry Morning Breakfast Cake

HAWTHORNE INN, CONCORD, MASSACHUSETTS

A stay at Hawthorne Inn becomes a lesson in eighteenth- and nineteenth-century American history, and innkeepers Gregory Burch and Marilyn Mudry have even prepared a suggested itinerary for a week's worth of exploring Concord and the surrounding area. Built in 1870, the inn occupies land once belonging to Ralph Waldo Emerson, the Alcotts, and Nathaniel Hawthorne. Guests are served an extensive continental breakfast, with homemade breads and home-grown raspberries and grapes among the offerings.

2 cups (4 sticks) butter, at room temperature

6 eggs

1 cup milk

1 heaping tablespoon baking powder

2 cups sugar

1 teaspoon pure vanilla extract

4 cups all-purpose flour

Juice of 1 lemon

2 tablespoons grated lemon rind

1 1/2 cups blueberries (or raspberries or blackberries)

1. Preheat the oven to 350 degrees F. Butter and flour one large and one small bundt pan.

2. Combine the butter, eggs, milk, baking powder, sugar, and vanilla in the bowl of a food processor and blend well.

3. Transfer the mixture to a large bowl and gradually add the flour, stirring well after each addition. Stir in the lemon juice, lemon rind, and berries and combine well. Spoon the batter into the prepared pans.

4. Bake for 1 1/4 hours or until a toothpick inserted in the center comes out clean. Cool in the pan for 30 minutes, then invert onto a rack to cool completely.

Serves 18 to 20.

Almond Coffee Cake

THE MAINSTAY INN, CAPE MAY, NEW JERSEY

*A raft of prestigious publications, including **Smithsonian** and **National Geographic Traveler**, have praised both the Italianate architecture and the superb hospitality of the Mainstay Inn, one of the most venerable lodgings in a town replete with possibilities for overnight stays. The **New York Times** once described innkeepers Sue and Tom Carroll as an 1880s couple in their 40s.*

Almond Filling

1 package (3 1/2 ounces) almond paste, cut up

 cup confectioners' sugar

1/4 cup (1/2 stick) margarine or butter

1/2 cup sliced almonds

Coffee Cake

1 1/2 cups sugar

3/4 cup (1 1/2 sticks) margarine or butter, at room temperature

1 1/2 teaspoons pure vanilla extract

3 eggs

3 cups all-purpose flour

1 1/2 teaspoons baking powder

1 1/2 teaspoons baking soda

3/4 teaspoon salt

1 1/2 cups sour cream

Glaze

1/2 cup confectioners' sugar

1/4 teaspoon pure vanilla extract

1 to 2 teaspoons milk

1. Preheat the oven to 325 degrees F. Grease a tube pan.

2. To prepare the almond filling, heat the almond paste, confectioners' sugar, and margarine over medium heat, stirring constantly, until smooth. Remove from the heat, stir in the almonds, and set aside.

3. Combine the sugar, margarine, vanilla, and eggs in the large bowl of an electric mixer and mix on medium speed for 2 minutes, scraping the bowl occasionally.

4. In a separate bowl, combine the flour, baking powder, baking soda, and salt.

5. Beat the flour mixture and the sour cream alternately into the egg mixture, using low speed. Spread one-third of the batter in the prepared pan. Sprinkle with one-third of the filling. Repeat twice.

6. Bake for 50 minutes, or until a toothpick inserted near the center comes out clean. Cool for 20 minutes and remove from the pan.

7. Combine the ingredients for the glaze and mix well. Drizzle over the coffee cake.

Makes 1 coffee cake.

Espresso Coffee Cake

VINTNERS INN, SANTA ROSA, CALIFORNIA

Guests at Vintners Inn are served a complimentary breakfast in the California style, and this imaginative coffee cake, devised by chefs Scott and Marge Noll, is often included. It freezes well, and the recipe may be doubled.

Cake

2 cups sifted all-purpose flour

1/2 teaspoon baking soda

1 teaspoon baking powder

1/4 teaspoon salt

3/4 cup (11/2 sticks) unsalted butter, at room temperature

1 cup sugar

2 eggs

2 teaspoons pure vanilla extract

1 cup sour cream

2 tablespoons instant espresso powder dissolved in 1 tablespoon hot water

Glaze

2 to 3 tablespoons hot, strong brewed coffee

11/2 teaspoons instant espresso powder

3/4 cup confectioners' sugar, sifted

1. Preheat the oven to 350 degrees F. Grease an 8-inch bundt pan.

2. Sift the flour, baking soda, baking powder, and salt into a small bowl.

3. In a large bowl, cream the butter and gradually add the sugar, beating until light and fluffy. Add the eggs, one at a time, beating well after each addition. Beat in the vanilla.

4. Add the flour mixture alternately with the sour cream, beginning and ending with flour and blending well after each addition.

5. Transfer about one-third of the batter to a small bowl and stir in the espresso and water mixture, stirring until well combined.

6. Spoon half of the plain batter into the prepared pan and spread evenly. Spoon the coffee batter over the plain batter and spread evenly. Top with the remaining plain batter and spread evenly.

7. Bake for 55 to 60 minutes or until golden and a toothpick tester comes out clean. Let cool in the pan for 30 minutes. Invert onto a rack and cool thoroughly.

8. To make the glaze, stir together the brewed coffee and the espresso powder until the powder is dissolved. Stir in the confectioners' sugar and mix well (add more brewed coffee if necessary to achieve pouring consistency). Pour the glaze over the cooled coffee cake and let stand for 10 minutes, or until the glaze is set.

Serves 8 to 10.

Desserts

Desserts

Chèvre Pound Cake

Pumpkin Pecan Cake

Bad, Bad Whiskey Cake

Chocolate Orange Drizzle Cake

White Chocolate Flourless Cake with Raspberry Coulis

Chocolate Hazelnut Torte

Chocolate Raspberry Truffle Cheesecake

Caramelized Apple Rum Custard Tart

Pear Tart

Southern Gardens Orange Pie

Lemon Sponge Pie

Crème Brûlée

Sugar Cone with Crème Anglaise and Berries

Ginger Custard

Rhubarb and Strawberry Compote

Red Lion Inn Cranberry Apple Crisp

Autumn Orchard Crisp

Banana Betty

Italian Plum Clafouti with Cognac

Brittle Maple Frango

Frozen Strawberry Soufflé with Chocolate Chantilly

Crispy Ice Cream Pie

Chocolate Pâté with Coconut Cream

Apricot Almond Dessert

Cinnamon Apple Bread Pudding

Warm French Bread Pudding

Indian Pudding

Chèvre Pound Cake

THE SQUIRE TARBOX INN, WISCASSET, MAINE

An engaging feature of the Squire Tarbox Inn is its small herd of Nubian goats, informally known as "the girls," whose milk is transformed into a variety of cheeses, served in many ways at the inn and marketed in the region. This simple pound cake is delicious as is or, as a special treat, garnished with fresh strawberries and whipped cream.

1/2 pound chèvre (goat cheese), at room temperature

1 1/2 cups (3 sticks) unsalted butter, at room temperature

2 cups sugar

Pinch of salt

1 1/2 teaspoons lemon extract or grated lemon rind

2 teaspoons pure vanilla extract

6 eggs, at room temperature

3 cups all-purpose flour

1. Preheat the oven to 325 degrees F. Butter and flour a 10-inch tube pan.

2. Cream the cheese and butter in an electric mixer. Add the sugar, salt, lemon extract, and vanilla extract and beat until the mixture is very light.

3. Add the eggs one by one and beat until the mixture is light and fluffy.

4. Reduce the speed of the mixer to low and add the flour, beating just until the ingredients are well combined.

5. Spoon the batter into the prepared pan and bake for 1 1/4 hours or until a toothpick inserted in the center comes out clean.

6. Remove the pan from the oven and let stand for 5 minutes. Invert the cake onto a rack and cool completely.

Serves 12 to 16.

Note: Cream cheese may be substituted for the chèvre.

Pumpkin Pecan Cake

THE GREY WHALE INN, FORT BRAGG, CALIFORNIA

One guest has compared the anticipation of the next day's breakfast at the Grey Whale Inn to Christmas Eve. This cake may be on the breakfast menu, but it is equally appropriate for lunch, dinner, or afternoon tea. Innkeeper Colette Bailey says, "As long as you have the ingredients out, you may as well make two cakes; they freeze well."

3 1/3 cups all-purpose flour

1/2 teaspoon baking powder

1 1/2 teaspoons salt

2 teaspoons baking soda

1 teaspoon ground cinnamon

1 teaspoon ground cloves

2/3 cup pecans, chopped in food processor

2/3 cup shortening

2 2/3 cups sugar

4 eggs, at room temperature

2 cups pumpkin purée

2/3 cup warm water

1. Preheat the oven to 350 degrees F. Grease and flour a 12-inch tube pan.

2. Place the flour, baking powder, salt, baking soda, cinnamon, and cloves in the bowl of a food processor and process until well combined. Transfer to a large mixing bowl and stir in the pecans.

3. Place the shortening and sugar in the food processor bowl and process until completely blended. Add the eggs and process for 20 seconds.

4. Beat the creamed mixture, the pumpkin purée, and the water into the dry ingredients until well blended. Spoon the batter into the prepared pan and bake for 1 hour or until a toothpick inserted in the center comes out clean.

5. Cool the cake on a rack for 10 minutes, then remove from the pan and continue cooling on the rack.

Serves 16.

Bad, Bad Whiskey Cake

COWSLIP'S BELLE BED AND BREAKFAST, ASHLAND, OREGON

Ashland is the home of the renowned Oregon Shakespeare Festival, and Cowslip's Belle takes its name from Midsummer Night's Dream, Act II, scene 1: "The cowslip's tall her pensioners be . . ." Each of the guest rooms is named for a flower mentioned in Shakespeare's plays, and, not surprisingly, cowslips (a kind of primrose) bloom in the owners' spring garden.

2 cups all-purpose flour

1/2 teaspoon salt

1 cup (2 sticks) unsalted butter, at room temperature

1 teaspoon pure vanilla extract

1/4 cup grated orange rind

13/4 cups sugar

5 eggs

1/4 cup milk

1/4 cup Irish whiskey

3/4 cup chopped pecans

Confectioners' sugar

1. Preheat the oven to 350 degrees F. Butter and flour a 9-inch bundt pan.

2. Sift the flour and salt together and set aside in a small bowl.

3. In a large bowl, beat the butter, vanilla extract, and orange rind until smooth. Gradually add the sugar, beating until blended.

4. Add the eggs one at a time and beat until fluffy and light.

5. Combine the milk and whiskey and add alternately with the flour to the butter and egg mixture, blending well after each addition. Stir in the pecans.

6. Pour the batter into the bundt pan and smooth the top to make a level surface. Bake for 1 hour or until a toothpick inserted in the center comes out clean.

7. Cool in the pan on a rack for about 15 minutes, then remove from the pan and continue to let stand on the rack until completely cool. Place on a cake plate or platter and dust with confectioners' sugar.

Serves 12.

Chocolate Orange Drizzle Cake

THE CAPTAIN'S HOUSE INN, CHATHAM, MASSACHUSETTS

Innkeeper Jan McMaster is a native of Bournemouth, England, and enjoys overseeing a proper English afternoon tea. This recipe, from the club known throughout England as the Women's Institute, has long been part of Jan's collection.

3/4 cup sugar

3/4 cup (1 1/2 sticks) butter, at room temperature

3 eggs, lightly beaten

Finely grated rind of 2 oranges

3/4 cup cake flour

Milk

Juice of 2 oranges, strained

1/4 cup sugar

Icing

1/2 cup confectioners' sugar

2 teaspoons unsweetened cocoa

Hot water

1. Preheat the oven to 350 degrees F. Grease a loaf pan and line it with wax paper; grease the paper.

2. Cream together the sugar and butter. Add the eggs and orange rind and stir until well combined. Lightly fold in the flour. Add enough milk to give the batter a soft dropping consistency.

3. Transfer the batter to the prepared pan, forming a slight hollow in the center of the top. Bake for about 55 minutes, until firm to the touch and the sides begin to pull away from the pan. Allow to cool in the pan for 5 minutes before turning out on a rack to cool.

4. Prepare a syrup by combining the orange juice and the 1/4 cup sugar in a small saucepan and heating over low heat until the sugar has dissolved.

5. When the cake is almost cold, make a series of shallow cuts across the top, then drizzle the orange syrup over it so that it soaks into the cake.

6. To prepare the Icing, dissolve the cocoa in a tablespoon of hot water. Sift the confectioners' sugar into a bowl and beat in the melted cocoa, adding more hot water until the proper consistency is achieved. Spread the icing over the top of the cake, allowing it to drip down the sides.

Serves 8 to 10.

White Chocolate Flourless Cake with Raspberry Coulis

STE. ANNE'S COUNTRY INN AND SPA, GRAFTON, ONTARIO

At Ste. Anne's, the Three R's are Rest, Relaxation, and Rejuvenation; and the inn's country setting and elaborate spa facilities allow guests to go straight to the head of the class. No matter how fitness-conscious one is by day, however, chef Curt Schmid's elegant desserts are hard to resist at dinnertime.

6 ounces white chocolate

3 tablespoons butter or margarine

8 eggs, separated

1/3 cup sugar

Raspberry Coulis (see recipe below)

1. Preheat the oven to 250 degrees F. Grease a 9-inch springform pan.

2. Melt the white chocolate and butter in the top of a double boiler over simmering water, using a whisk to combine well. Set aside.

3. Place the egg yolks in a bowl and beat well. Fold in the chocolate mixture.

4. In another bowl, whip the egg whites to soft peaks; add the sugar.

5. Fold one-fourth of the egg whites into the yolk mixture and combine well. Carefully fold in the remaining egg whites. Pour into the prepared pan and bake for 1 1/4 hours.

6. Remove the cake from the oven. Using a sharp knife, carefully cut around the edge of the pan. Allow the cake to cool to room temperature.

7. To serve, remove the sides of the pan and cut the cake into serving pieces with a serrated knife. Drizzle a small amount of Raspberry Coulis onto individual serving plates and place a wedge of cake on top.

Serves 12.

Raspberry Coulis

1 cup frozen raspberries
1/4 cup sugar
2 teaspoons fresh lemon juice

1. Place the raspberries, sugar, and lemon juice in a small saucepan and bring to a simmer over low heat. Cook until the sugar is dissolved.

2. Purée the mixture in a blender, then strain through a sieve. Refrigerate, covered, until ready to use.

Makes about 1 cup.

Chocolate Hazelnut Torte

SHERWOOD INN, SKANEATELES, NEW YORK

Skaneateles is one of the loveliest towns in the Finger Lakes region of central New York state, and its Sherwood Inn has been a favorite resting place for travelers since Isaac Sherwood built a stagecoach stop in 1807. In the 1820s it was a way station for coach tours en route to Niagara Falls from New York City, and with the advent of the train, the inn hosted excursionists arriving at the lake for extended summer visits. Today the Sherwood Inn attracts travelers and local residents alike, with upscale American cuisine the bill of fare.

1 cup unsweetened cocoa

1 1/2 cups boiling water

4 eggs

1 tablespoon pure vanilla extract

3 1/2 cups cake flour

2 1/4 cups sugar

1 teaspoon baking soda

1 teaspoon salt

1 1/2 cups (3 sticks) unsalted butter, at room temperature

3/4 cup chopped hazelnuts

Whipped Ganache Frosting (see recipe below)

1. Preheat the oven to 350 degrees F. Grease two 9 x 1 1/2-inch cake pans, line with parchment paper, and grease and flour the paper.

2. In a small bowl, whisk together the cocoa and boiling water. Let cool to room temperature.

3. In a mixing bowl, beat together the eggs, one-fourth of the cocoa mixture, and the vanilla extract.

4. In the bowl of an electric mixer, combine the flour, sugar, baking soda, and salt and mix on low speed for 30 seconds. Add the butter and the remaining cocoa mixture and combine well on low speed. Beat on medium speed for 1 1/2 minutes. Scrape down the sides. By hand, fold in the hazelnuts.

5. Add the egg mixture in three batches, beating by hand for 20 seconds after each addition.

6. Transfer the batter to the prepared pans and bake for 20 to 30 minutes, or until a cake tester comes out clean and the center of the cake springs back. Cool for 10 minutes on a wire rack, then remove from pans and let cool to room temperature. Transfer the cake layers to plates and chill.

7. Frost the chilled layers with Whipped Ganache Frosting.

Serves 10 to 12.

Whipped Ganache Frosting

8 ounces semisweet chocolate
2 cups heavy cream
1/2 teaspoon pure vanilla extract

1. Melt the chocolate in the top of a double boiler over simmering water. Heat the cream and vanilla extract in a saucepan until very warm but not boiling.

2. Add the cream to the chocolate, beat until well blended, and chill for about 2 hours. Beat at high speed until soft peaks form, then frost the chilled torte layers.

Makes about 2 1/2 cups.

Chocolate Raspberry Truffle Cheesecake

ROWELL'S INN, SIMONSVILLE (CHESTER), VERMONT

Lee and Beth Davis refer to themselves as "keepers of the inn," and speak of their establishment in unabashedly old-fashioned terms. "During the mid–1900s the inn was oft remembered as a preferred luncheon stop on the 'Ideal Tour' between Manchester, Vermont, and the White Mountains of New Hampshire for hearty fare of trout and chicken and the sweet temptation of homemade pies."

2 1/2 cups chocolate wafer crumbs

1/3 cup melted butter

1/2 cup plus 1 cup sugar

8 ounces semisweet chocolate, cut into 1/2-inch cubes

1/4 cup hot strong coffee

3 8-ounce packages cream cheese

1 cup sour cream

2 eggs

2 tablespoons heavy cream

1 teaspoon pure vanilla extract

1/4 cup Chambord liqueur

Raspberry Sauce

1 10-ounce package frozen raspberries, thawed

2 teaspoons cornstarch

1. Preheat the oven to 350 degrees F.

2. Combine the wafer crumbs with the melted butter and the 1/2 cup sugar and mix well. Press the mixture onto the bottom and 1 1/2 inches up the sides of a 9-inch springform pan. Set aside.

3. Place the chocolate cubes in the bowl of a food processor and process until finely ground. With the motor running, pour in the hot coffee and process until the chocolate is melted.

4. Add the cream cheese, sour cream, 1 cup sugar, eggs, heavy cream, vanilla extract, and Chambord and process until the mixture is smooth, stopping to scrape the sides when needed.

5. Pour the mixture into the prepared pan and bake for 55 minutes (the center will be soft). Let cool to room temperature, cover, and chill for at least 8 hours.

6. To prepare the Raspberry Sauce, drain the raspberries, reserving the juice. Combine the juice and the cornstarch in a small saucepan and cook over medium heat, stirring, until smooth and thickened. Cool. Press the berries through a sieve and add the purée to the cooled sauce.

7. Pool a small amount of sauce on each serving plate and top with a wedge of cheesecake.

Serves 8 to 10.

Caramelized Apple Rum Custard Tart

THE INN AT THORN HILL, JACKSON, NEW HAMPSHIRE

*The calendar at Thorn Hill is punctuated with special events year-round,
starting with a Spring Fling dinner in early May, continuing on to a Harvest
Moon Celebration in September, and ending the year with November's
Nouveau Beaujolais Wine Dinner and a Holiday Open House in December.
On all these occasions—and every day—the air is filled with the aromas of
gourmet cooking. Orders are individually prepared, and all the pastries are
made on the premises.*

4 apples, peeled, cored, and sliced

1/4 cup plus 1 cup sugar

2 tablespoons fresh lemon juice

6 tablespoons (3/4 stick) unsalted butter

Pinch of salt

1 egg

1 egg yolk

2 tablespoons 80-proof dark rum

1 cup milk

2 tablespoons sugar

Pâte Brisée (see recipe below)

Ground cinnamon

1. Preheat the oven to 325 degrees F.

2. Toss the apples in the 1/4 cup sugar and the lemon juice, place in
   a sieve set over a bowl, and allow to drain for 20 minutes (discard
   the juice).

3. Melt the butter in a heavy saucepan, add the 1 cup sugar and cook
   over medium heat until the mixture turns golden brown (there may
   be lumps). Add the apples and cook, covered, for 5 minutes and
   uncovered for another 5 minutes.

4. Remove the apples and arrange in a baked pâte brisée shell.

5. Combine the salt, egg, egg yolk, rum, milk, and 2 tablespoons sugar
   and beat well. Pour over the apples and bake until set, about 30
   minutes. Dust with cinnamon and serve immediately.

Pâte Brisée

1 1/4 cups all-purpose flour
6 tablespoons (3/4 stick) cold butter, cut in pieces
2 tablespoons cold vegetable shortening, cut in pieces
1/4 teaspoon salt
1 tablespoon sugar
Ice water

1. Place the flour, butter, shortening, salt, and sugar in the bowl of a food processor and process until the mixture resembles fine meal.

2. Gradually add ice water, just until the mixture forms a ball.

3. Remove the dough from the processor and knead lightly for a few seconds. Flatten slightly to form a disc and chill, wrapped in plastic wrap, for 1 hour before rolling out.

Makes 1 9-inch crust.

Pear Tart

FOUR COLUMNS INN, NEWFANE, VERMONT

This recipe comes from the family collection of innkeepers Jacques and Pamela Allembert. The goal is to arrange the pears so that the final design resembles a lovely blossom. The flavors of the tart will be equally lovely.

Crust

2/3 cup sugar

11/2 cups plus 2 tablespoons (13/4 sticks) butter

2 cups all-purpose flour

1/2 teaspoon pure vanilla extract

Filling

4 3-ounce packages cream cheese

1/2 cup sugar

1/2 teaspoon vanilla extract

2 eggs, lightly beaten

Topping

8 to 10 red Bartlett pears, or a juicy equivalent, peeled, cored, and sliced

3 tablespoons sugar

1 teaspoon ground cinnamon

1/2 teaspoon ground nutmeg

1/2 to 3/4 cup sliced raw almonds

1. Preheat the oven to 350 degrees F.

2. In a large bowl, combine the ingredients for the crust, cutting the butter in with a pastry blender or two knives until the mixture is crumbly. Line the bottom and partway up the sides of a springform pan with the crust mixture.

3. To prepare the filling, place all the ingredients in a large bowl and beat well.

4. To assemble the tart, pour the filling into the crust and arrange the pears over the filling in concentric circles, to form a blossom.

5. Combine the sugar, cinnamon, and nutmeg in a small bowl and sprinkle the mixture over the pear slices. Top with the sliced almonds.

6. Bake the tart for 45 minutes to 1 hour, until the pears are soft.

Serves 8 to 10.

Southern Gardens Orange Pie

CLEWISTON INN, CLEWISTON, FLORIDA

This recipe was created by the Clewiston Inn to serve at the formal opening of the United States Sugar Corporation's Southern Gardens Citrus plant in 1994 and quickly became a favorite on the inn's menu.

1 8-ounce package cream cheese, at room temperature

1/2 cup frozen orange juice concentrate, thawed

1 teaspoon orange flavoring

2 teaspoons grated orange rind

1/2 cup orange sections

1 14-ounce can sweetened condensed milk

1 3 3/8-ounce package instant vanilla pudding

2 tablespoons fresh lemon juice

1 9-inch cookie crumb pie shell

1 cup heavy cream

1. In a large bowl beat the cream cheese until smooth. Add the remaining ingredients, except the pie shell and the heavy cream, and mix well.

2. Spoon the mixture into the pie shell and refrigerate until set. Before serving, whip the cream and spread it over the pie.

Serves 6 to 8.

Lemon Sponge Pie

HICKORY BRIDGE FARM, ORRTANNA, PENNSYLVANIA

The food served for dinner and breakfast at Hickory Bridge Farm is best described as wholesome, prepared with fresh local ingredients and incorporating the traditions of the Pennsylvania Dutch region in which it is located. Many of the recipes have been handed down through four generations of the Hammet and Martin families, who share the innkeeping. This one is a typical Pennsylvania Dutch dessert.

2 tablespoons vegetable shortening

1 cup sugar

1/2 teaspoon salt

3 tablespoons flour

2 eggs, separated

1 cup milk

1/4 cup fresh lemon juice

1 tablespoon grated lemon rind

1 unbaked 9-inch pie shell

1. Preheat the oven to 375 degrees F.

2. Place the shortening, sugar, and salt in a mixing bowl and cream until light and fluffy. Beat in the flour.

3. In a separate bowl, beat the egg yolks and blend in the milk and lemon juice. Add to the creamed mixture with the lemon rind.

4. In another bowl, beat the egg whites until stiff peaks form. Fold the egg whites into the lemon mixture until just incorporated.

5. Pour the mixture into the pie shell and bake for 10 minutes. Reduce the oven temperature to 350 degrees F and continue baking for 35 minutes, or until the center is set.

Serves 6.

Crème Brûlée

NATHANIEL PORTER INN, WARREN, RHODE ISLAND

The restoration of what was once known as the "mansion house" turned up several exceptionally fine examples of early decorative arts. In one of the three dining rooms there is a bold leaf-patterned stenciling that is one of the earliest patterns documented in America. Another dining room has murals replicating the traces of ca. 1810 paysage panoramique *wall covering found during the restoration.*

4 cups heavy cream

10 egg yolks

1 cup sugar

1 1/2 teaspoons pure vanilla extract

1 pint blueberries, strawberries, or raspberries (optional)

1/2 cup light brown sugar

1. Heat the cream in a heavy saucepan over low heat until very hot but not boiling.

2. In a stainless steel mixing bowl, beat the egg yolks and the sugar until the mixture is pale yellow. Pour the hot cream into the egg yolks a little at a time, whisking constantly.

3. Place the mixing bowl over a pot of boiling water and continue to whisk the mixture until it is thickened, about 15 minutes. The mixture should come to a slight boil. Add the vanilla extract.

4. Divide the berries among eight 6-ounce custard cups. Pour the custard mixture over the berries and set aside to cool. Cover and refrigerate for at least 5 hours or up to 2 days.

5. Preheat the broiler. Sprinkle each custard with a tablespoon of brown sugar and place under the broiler until the tops are brown, about 1 minute. The brown sugar will form a crisp crust. (Be careful not to overcook, as brown sugar burns quickly.) Serve immediately.

Serves 8 to 10.

Note: If you use berries, the custard mixture will go farther and will probably fill ten custard cups.

Sugar Cone with Crème Anglaise and Berries

THE BIRD & BOTTLE INN, GARRISON, NEW YORK

At the Bird & Bottle, this elegant dessert is served with the Crème Anglaise pooled on the plate and "overpainted" with a cobweb design of raspberry purée. Without the painting, the dish will still impress your most sophisticated guests.

Sugar Cone

1/2 cup flour

1/3 cup sugar

1 egg

1 teaspoon pure vanilla extract

Crème Anglaise

2 cups light cream

1 vanilla bean, split

6 egg yolks

1/4 cup sugar

Berries (your choice of raspberries, blueberries, blackberries)

Fresh mint sprigs

1. Preheat the oven to 350 degrees F. Grease a baking sheet, line with parchment paper, and grease the paper.

2. To make the Sugar Cones, blend the flour, sugar, egg, and vanilla extract in a bowl. Make 4 cookies (using 1 tablespoonful of dough for each one) on each sheet (prepare more than one baking sheet or use the same one for three batches). Using the back of a tablespoon, spread out the dough to make a 4-inch circle. Bake for 4 to 8 minutes, until light brown. While the cookies are hot, roll into cone shape. Let cool. Continue the process until you have made 12 cones.

3. To make the Crème Anglaise, heat the cream with the vanilla bean until hot but not boiling.

4. In a bowl, beat together the egg yolks and sugar until thick and lemon-colored.

5. Remove the cream from the heat, whisk it into the yolk mixture, return to the heat, and cook, stirring, for 5 to 7 minutes (do not boil). Strain the mixture, cover, and refrigerate for 2 to 3 hours.

6. To assemble the dessert, pool some Crème Anglaise on 9-inch dessert plates. Scatter berries over the Crème Anglaise. Top with a sugar cone and place additional berries at the open end, cascading out of the cone. Garnish with a mint sprig.

Serves 6 or 12 (depending on whether you serve one or two cones to each guest).

Ginger Custard

WINDHAM HILL INN, WEST TOWNSHEND, VERMONT

Windham Hill has a quiet country setting in south central Vermont, with 160 acres of meadow and forest for hiking and cross-country skiing. The dress code is "comfortable" and the food is described as elegant-yet-approachable. This custard may be served as is or inverted onto individual plates and accompanied by crème Anglaise or raspberry purée and wild berries.

1 quart half-and-half

1 cup sugar

1 tablespoon grated fresh ginger root (peeled)

4 eggs

5 egg yolks

2 tablespoons Cointreau or Amaretto liqueur (optional)

1. Preheat the oven to 350 degrees F.

2. In a saucepan, heat the half-and-half, sugar, and ginger root until the mixture is warm.

3. In a bowl, beat the eggs and egg yolks for 2 minutes. Gradually add the warm cream to the eggs. Stir in the liqueur.

4. Strain the mixture through a fine sieve and fill twelve ramekins. Place the ramekins in a large baking pan and surround with hot water to reach halfway up the sides of the ramekins. Cover the baking pan with foil and bake for 30 minutes or until set.

Serves 12.

Rhubarb and Strawberry Compote

ANGEL OF THE SEA BED AND BREAKFAST, CAPE MAY, NEW JERSEY

The meal of the day at Angel of the Sea is breakfast, featuring a sumptuous buffet of cold fruits, cereals, and homemade breads as well as a choice of hot entrées cooked to order. In season, this compote is often part of the array, though it works equally well as an early summer dessert.

1/2 cup water

1 cup sugar

1 2-inch piece ginger root, peeled and quartered

1 pound rhubarb, peeled and cut into 1½-inch pieces

1 tablespoon grated orange rind

1 pint strawberries, hulled and halved

1 tablespoon Kirsch liqueur (optional)

Heavy cream

1. Bring the water, sugar, and ginger to a boil in a heavy saucepan over medium heat. Add the rhubarb, return the mixture to a boil, lower the heat, and simmer for 3 to 4 minutes, partially covered. The rhubarb should be soft but retain its shape.

2. Remove the fruit from the heat and gently stir in the orange rind. Let cool to room temperature.

3. Stir in the strawberries and Kirsch. Chill.

4. Remove the ginger and serve topped with heavy cream.

Serves 8.

Red Lion Cranberry Apple Crisp

THE RED LION INN, STOCKBRIDGE, MASSACHUSETTS

Chef Steve Mongeon, who has presided over the kitchen at the Red Lion Inn for over ten years, describes the inn's menu as traditional New England fare, but of the 1990s—not two hundred years ago. "We've adapted traditional New England recipes for today's healthy attitudes." Though this recipe may not have seen many changes over the years, the oats are definitely of the '90s.

1 cup rolled oats
1 cup all-purpose flour
1 cup light brown sugar, firmly packed
1/4 teaspoon baking soda
1/4 teaspoon baking powder
1/4 teaspoon salt
1/2 cup (1 stick) butter, melted
3 1/2 pounds (about 7 large) tart apples, peeled, cored, and sliced
1/2 cup fresh cranberries
3/4 cup sugar
1 1/2 teaspoons ground cinnamon

1. Preheat the oven to 450 degrees F. Lightly butter an 8 x 8-inch square pan.

2. Combine the dry ingredients for the topping and stir in the melted butter.

3. Place the apples and cranberries in a large bowl and toss to combine. Add the sugar and cinnamon and toss again.

4. Thinly cover the bottom of the prepared pan with one-third of the topping mixture, pressing it down.

5. Pour in the fruit and cover with the remaining topping mixture. Cover the pan with aluminum foil and bake for 1 1/4 hours, or until the apples are tender, removing the foil during the last quarter hour of cooking to allow the top to brown.

Serves 8 to 10.

Autumn Orchard Crisp

GREENVILLE ARMS 1889 INN, GREENVILLE, NEW YORK

In 1889 William Vanderbilt designed and built a beautiful country home in the Catskills in the fashionable Queen Anne style. The residence was converted to an inn in 1952, and today innkeepers Eliot and Letitia Dalton pride themselves on contributing to a tradition of old-fashioned hospitality. Possible day trips from the inn extend from Cooperstown to West Point to Saratoga Springs, with many points of interest in between.

3 pounds firm, flavorful apples
1 pound pears
Juice of 1/2 lemon
3 tablespoons granulated sugar
1 cup light brown sugar
1 cup all-purpose flour
2 tablespoons ground cinnamon
1/2 cup (1 stick) butter, at room temperature, cut up
1 1/2 cups chopped walnuts
1/2 cup coarsely chopped cranberries
Whipped cream or vanilla ice cream

1. Preheat the oven to 350 degrees F. Butter a 13 x 9-inch baking pan.

2. Peel, core, and slice the apples and pears and toss them in a bowl with the lemon juice and granulated sugar.

3. Place the brown sugar, flour, cinnamon, butter, and half the nuts in the bowl of a food processor. Process until blended and crumbly.

4. Spread one-third of the crumb mixture on the bottom of the prepared pan, top with half of the sliced fruit and scatter over half of the cranberries. Top with the second third of the crumb mixture.

5. Layer on the remaining sliced fruit and sprinkle over the remaining cranberries. Mix the remaining nuts with the remaining crumb mixture and spread over the top.

6. Bake until well browned and slightly bubbly, about 1 hour.
Cool to warm and top with whipped cream or ice cream.

Serves 8.

Banana Betty

BEEKMAN ARMS, RHINEBECK, NEW YORK

The historic authenticity of a 200-year-old inn, where General Washington and his troops drilled on the front lawn, combines with the best of contemporary American cuisine to make the Beekman Arms an especially satisfying experience. In this recipe, the betty of bygone days gets an up-to-the-minute interpretation.

1 cup gingersnap crumbs

3 or 4 small bananas

1 1/3 cups heavy cream

3 egg yolks

1/4 cup sugar

Pure vanilla extract to taste

Dark rum to taste

1. Butter four 6-ounce ramekins.

2. Sift the gingersnap crumbs and sprinkle 1 teaspoon into each of the prepared ramekins. Reserve the remaining crumbs.

3. Slice the bananas into 1/4-inch slices and place in the ramekins to make the containers three-fourths full.

4. Bring the cream to a boil in a heavy saucepan. Remove from the heat.

5. Whisk together the egg yolks and sugar and add half of the hot cream to the mixture. Whisk together well. Pour the mixture back into the remaining hot cream and whisk until thoroughly incorporated.

6. Place the pan over medium heat and cook, stirring, until the mixture reaches 180 degrees F on a candy thermometer. Strain and flavor with vanilla and rum.

7. Pour the custard over the bananas, filling each ramekin. Push the bananas down to assure complete coverage. Cover with plastic wrap and chill overnight.

8. Top the chilled ramekins with the remaining gingersnap crumbs, scraping with a straightedge to make a level top. Bring the ramekins to room temperature and then warm in a 350 degree F oven for 5 to 7 minutes. Serve warm.

Serves 4.

Italian Plum Clafouti with Cognac

THE CHECKERBERRY INN, GOSHEN, INDIANA

Though innkeepers John and Susan Graff are natives of Goshen and in 1987 decided to build their inn in familiar territory, another part of their life is spent on the island of Anguilla, where they own a home and a group of seaside villas. Thus the Checkerberry Inn reflects a combination of local and cosmopolitan influences—European objects accent the comfortable décor, and the menu combines French country cuisine with Amish simplicity.

1 cup milk

1/3 cup heavy cream

3 eggs

2 teaspoons pure vanilla extract

2 tablespoons Cognac

1/3 cup plus 4 tablespoons sugar

2 teaspoons finely minced lemon rind

3/4 cup all-purpose flour

Pinch of salt

15 ripe Italian plums, pitted and quartered

Whipped cream (optional)

1. Preheat the oven to 375 degrees F. Butter a 10 x 11/2-inch tart or pie pan (without a removable bottom).

2. Place the milk, cream, eggs, vanilla extract, and Cognac in the bowl of a food processor and process until combined.

3. Mix the 1/3 cup sugar, 1 teaspoon of the lemon rind, the flour, and salt in a small bowl. Add to the food processor and process until smooth. There should be about 3 cups of batter.

4. Pour 11/2 cups batter into the prepared pan. Arrange the plum quarters on top in one layer. Sprinkle with the remaining lemon rind and gently pour the rest of the batter over the plums. Bake for 15 minutes.

5. Remove from the oven, sprinkle with the 4 tablespoons of sugar and bake for 45 minutes more, or until the center is set and the top is puffed and brown. (If the center is set but the top has not browned, put the pan under the broiler for 1 to 2 minutes.)

6. Let cool on a wire rack for 5 minutes, cut into wedges, and serve warm with softly whipped cream. (The puffed look will diminish as the clafouti cools.)

Serves 6.

Brittle Maple Frango

LOWELL INN, STILLWATER, MINNESOTA

The alaga syrup called for in this recipe is similar to molasses and is easy to find in grocery stores in the South. For the rest of us, an additional quarter cup of maple syrup will produce perfectly acceptable results. The chef at Lowell Inn also suggests the possible addition of a smattering of liqueur—macadamia nut, hazelnut, whatever appeals.

3/4 cup maple syrup
1/4 cup Alaga syrup
4 egg yolks, at room temperature
3 cups heavy cream
Chocolate sauce, for garnish
Chopped Heath Bars, for garnish

1. Warm the syrups slightly over low heat. Beat the syrups into the egg yolks and cook, stirring constantly, in a heavy saucepan (or in the top of a double boiler over hot water) until the mixture thickens. Let cool.

2. Whip the cream in a large bowl. Fold in the maple mixture.

3. Pour the mixture into an oiled 9 x 5-inch loaf pan and freeze until firm. Slice and serve topped with a small amount of chocolate sauce and a sprinkling of chopped toffee bars.

Serves 8 to 10.

Frozen Strawberry Soufflé with Chocolate Chantilly

NORTH HERO HOUSE, NORTH HERO, VERMONT

After a day on the waters of Lake Champlain the evening meal takes on great importance, and chef Jack Sherlock never disappoints. This sophisticated dessert complements the casual surroundings in truly delicious fashion.

1/3 cup water

3/4 cup sugar

1 quart fresh ripe strawberries or raspberries

1 cup heavy cream

Cocoa powder, for garnish

Chocolate Chantilly

4 tablespoons cocoa powder (see note below)

1 cup heavy cream

1 tablespoon sugar

1. Form collars around eight individual soufflé dishes by tying a strip of stiff paper or aluminum foil around the top, letting it rise 2 inches above the rim of the dish. Oil the inside of the collar.

2. Bring the water and sugar to a boil in a heavy saucepan and boil until the sugar completely dissolves. Let cool.

3. Purée the strawberries and sugar syrup in a blender. Add the cream and blend until firm but not stiff. Transfer the mixture to a bowl large enough to leave at least an inch of space at the top. Freeze until half frozen.

4. Whip the half-frozen mixture and spoon into the prepared soufflé dishes. Freeze.

5. At serving time, prepare the Chocolate Chantilly by beating the cocoa, heavy cream, and sugar until stiff.

6. Remove the paper collars from the soufflé dishes. Place a dollop of the Chocolate Chantilly atop each soufflé and sprinkle with a little dry cocoa.

Serves 8.

Note: Be sure to use a cocoa that will dissolve in cold liquid.

Crispy Ice Cream Pie

ROCKHOUSE MOUNTAIN FARM-INN, EATON CENTER, NEW HAMPSHIRE

Elizabeth Edge and her family have been providing farm vacations since 1946, and no inn is more welcoming to children of all ages. Saturday night steak roasts on the back lawn, chicken barbecues at the Old Maple Sugar House, and weekly hayrides for the kids are just some of the activities sure to please the younger members of the family. And a favorite dessert among this set is Crispy Ice Cream Pie. The flavors for filling and topping are up to you and your family. The Edges like vanilla or strawberry ice cream topped with crushed fresh strawberries.

1 tablespoon margarine
2/3 cup marshmallow cream
2 1/2 cups Rice Krispies cereal
1 1/2 pints ice cream
Fresh fruit or prepared topping

1. Butter a 9-inch pie pan.

2. Melt the margarine in a large frying pan. Remove from the heat and whisk in the marshmallow cream.

3. Add the cereal and mix until it is completely coated with the marshmallow mixture. Press the mixture into the prepared pan, using your knuckles to flatten it and to build up the sides of the crust. Chill for about 45 minutes.

4. Fill the chilled crust with your choice of ice cream. Freeze until firm.

5. Top with fresh fruit or a sauce.

Serves 6 to 8.

Chocolate Pâté with Coconut Cream

STAFFORDS-IN-THE-FIELD, CHOCORUA, NEW HAMPSHIRE

The Staffords' country dining room, lighted by the cozy glow of kerosene finger lamps, has a menu with decidedly city characteristics. As is the case in so many country inns, fresh ingredients from the immediate vicinity are used by artful chefs to create a cuisine that marries rural and urban in a most successful way.

15 ounces bittersweet chocolate, chopped

4 tablespoons (1/2 stick) unsalted butter

1 cup heavy cream

4 egg yolks

3/4 cup confectioners' sugar

6 tablespoons Armagnac

Coconut Cream

1 1/2 cups light cream

1 cup shredded sweetened coconut

5 egg yolks

1/4 to 1/2 cup sugar, to taste

Pinch of salt

1/4 teaspoon pure vanilla extract

4 tablespoons Cointreau

1. Line a 9 x 5-inch loaf pan with parchment paper or wax paper, leaving enough paper hanging over the sides to be able to cover the top.

2. Melt the chocolate, butter, and cream in a heavy saucepan over low heat; stir until smooth. Remove from the heat.

3. Whisk the egg yolks into the chocolate one at a time, beating well after each addition. Whisk in the confectioners' sugar and beat until the mixture is smooth and glossy. Stir in the Armagnac.

4. Pour the mixture into the prepared pan and chill or freeze.

5. To make the Coconut Cream, scald the cream in a heavy saucepan. Remove from the heat, add the coconut and let cool. Strain off and discard the coconut.

6. In a mixing bowl, beat the egg yolks with the sugar, salt, and vanilla extract.

7. Reheat the cream and slowly whisk the hot cream into the egg mixture. Place the mixture in the top of a double boiler and cook, stirring, over hot water until it thickens. Remove from the heat, strain, and add the Cointreau. Place plastic wrap directly on the surface of the sauce as it cools, to keep a skin from forming.

8. Slice the pâté and serve with the sauce.

Serves 8 to 10.

Note: The pâté freezes well and may be sliced directly from the freezer. The Coconut Cream will hold in the refrigerator for about a week.

Apricot Almond Dessert

PHILBROOK FARM INN, SHELBURNE, NEW HAMPSHIRE

At Philbrook Farm, where guests are considered extended family, one finds simplicity instead of luxury and genuineness rather than pretense. Fresh local ingredients and family recipes are the order of the day. This recipe was supplied by a cousin of the Philbrooks and has made a big hit. It's easy to prepare ahead and keep on hand in the freezer.

1 1/2 cups vanilla wafer crumbs
1/3 cup melted butter
2/3 cup toasted chopped almonds
1 teaspoon pure vanilla extract
1/2 gallon vanilla ice cream, softened
1 10-ounce jar apricot jam

1. Butter a 9 x 9-inch square pan.

2. Combine the wafer crumbs, butter, almonds, and vanilla extract and mix well.

3. Pat half the crumb mixture onto the bottom of the prepared pan. Reserve the remaining crumb mixture.

4. Spread the ice cream over the crumbs. Freeze until firm.

5. Quickly spread the jam over the firm ice cream and cover with the reserved crumb mixture. Cover and freeze. Remove from the freezer 20 minutes before serving. Cut into squares.

Serves 9.

Cinnamon Apple Bread Pudding

THE AMERICAN GRILL AT CREEKWOOD, MICHIGAN CITY, INDIANA

Hot chocolate before bedtime is a chilly-weather tradition at Creekwood, just one of the examples of gracious service provided by innkeepers Mary Lou Linnen and Peggie Wall. The grounds of the inn have trails for cross-country skiing in winter or hiking in summer.

1 loaf stale Italian or French bread, crusts removed

1 cup apple sauce

1 cup raisins

6 eggs

2 cups milk

1 cup sugar

1 cup heavy cream

1 cup apple cider

1 teaspoon pure vanilla extract

1 tablespoon ground cinnamon

Glaze

1 cup sugar

1 tablespoon ground cinnamon

1/4 cup hot water

1. Preheat the oven to 325 degrees F. Grease a 9-inch springform pan and wrap aluminum foil around the bottom of the outside of the pan.

2. Cut the bread into cubes (you should have 4 cups). Place half the bread cubes in the bottom of the prepared pan. Spoon the apple sauce over the bread and sprinkle with the raisins. Top with the remaining bread cubes.

3. In a large bowl, lightly beat the eggs. Whisk in the milk, sugar, cream, and cider. Add the vanilla extract and cinnamon. Pour the mixture over the bread and let sit for 5 minutes to allow the bread to absorb the liquid.

4. To prepare the glaze, mix together the sugar and cinnamon; add hot water to form a paste. Drizzle the glaze over the bread and bake for 45 minutes.

Serves 8 to 10.

Warm French Bread Pudding

COBBLE HOUSE INN, GAYSVILLE, VERMONT

Owner/chef Beau Benson varies this dessert with the time of year, using whatever fruits are in season. She recommends firm fruits, such as tart green apples, peaches, pineapple, raisins. Those guests who aren't counting calories enjoy the pudding topped with a scoop of Vermont's favorite ice cream—Ben and Jerry's.

1/2 cup (1 stick) butter, at room temperature

1 cup superfine sugar

6 eggs

1 3/4 cups milk

2 teaspoons pure vanilla extract

1/2 teaspoon ground nutmeg

1/2 teaspoon ground cinnamon

6 cups cubed sourdough French bread

1 1/2 cups cubed fruit

1/2 cup maple syrup

1. Preheat the oven to 350 degrees F. Butter a 2-quart baking dish.

2. Cream the butter and sugar in a large bowl. Add the eggs one at a time, beating after each addition. Stir in the milk, vanilla extract, nutmeg, and cinnamon. The mixture will look grainy.

3. Add the bread cubes and the fruit to the mixture, toss, and let stand for 10 minutes.

4. Pour the mixture into the prepared baking dish and cover with aluminum foil. Bake for 40 minutes. Uncover and bake for 10 more minutes.

5. Remove the pudding from the oven and drizzle with the maple syrup. Serve hot or warm.

Serves 8 to 10.

Indian Pudding

THE VERMONT INN, KILLINGTON, VERMONT

Any recipe-gathering project experiences a number of duplications, and for this book the prizewinner for repeat submissions is Indian pudding. It seems appropriate, therefore, to end the dessert collection with this all-time country inn favorite (and not just in New England!).

1½ cups cornmeal

2 quarts milk

½ pound raisins

1 teaspoon ground ginger

1 teaspoon ground cinnamon

1 teaspoon ground nutmeg

1 teaspoon salt

3 eggs

1 cup molasses

½ pound light brown sugar

1. Combine the cornmeal, milk, and raisins in the top of a large double boiler and cook over simmering water until thickened. Remove from heat.

2. Preheat the oven to 350 degrees F. Butter a 13 x 9-inch baking dish.

3. Combine the remaining ingredients in a large bowl. Slowly stir a small amount of the hot mixture into the egg/sugar mixture, whisking briskly, until the egg/sugar mixture is warm to the touch. Then stir all of the egg/sugar mixture into the remainder of the hot mixture, blending well.

4. Pour into the prepared baking dish and bake for 45 minutes, or until set. Serve warm, with a small scoop of vanilla ice cream.

Serves 8 to 10.

Country Inn Potpourri

Country Inn Potpourri

Taffy's Peach Chutney
Warm Vidalia Onion and Summer Cherry Compote
Compote of Dried Fruits
Brandied Pear Butter
Liz's Pear Preserves
Rosé Punch
Lib's Almond Punch
Avocado Dill Dressing
Branded Onion Vinaigrette
Country Ham Salad
Tomato, Cheese, and Pesto Croûtons

Taffy's Peach Chutney

1810 WEST INN, THOMSON, GEORGIA

Virginia White has created a compound of historic buildings to house her ten-room bed-and-breakfast inn just thirty miles from Augusta. The main house, built in 1810 entirely of heart of pine, has intricate moldings not usually found in this part of Georgia as well as six fireplaces and antique furnishings. Behind the main house are two tenant houses from the area, moved to the property and restored for use as guest cottages.

8 large peaches, ripe but firm (to measure 6 cups of chunks)
3/4 cup raisins
2 cups firmly packed light brown sugar
3/4 cup cider vinegar
1/2 teaspoon salt
1 cup flaked coconut
1/2 cup chopped candied ginger
3/4 teaspoon Tabasco sauce
2 teaspoons mustard seed
2 small onions, chopped fine

1. Peel the peaches and cut into chunks. Combine with the remaining ingredients in a large saucepan.

2. Cook over low heat, stirring frequently, until the peaches are tender and the mixture is thick, about 1 hour.

3. Ladle the mixture into hot, sterilized jars and seal.

Makes 3 pints.

Warm Vidalia Onion and Summer Cherry Compote

L'ÉTOILE AT THE CHARLOTTE INN, EDGARTOWN, MASSACHUSETTS

The dining room at l'étoile is a glass-enclosed patio decorated with antiques and paintings, with French doors opening onto an eating area in the garden. Summer is the high season on Martha's Vineyard, and Edgartown is the hub— not only for yachtsmen and second home owners but for tourists and even daytrippers. This compote is a refreshing accompaniment to cold meats for a light summer meal.

2 cups thinly sliced Vidalia onions
1/3 cup olive oil
1/4 cup honey
1/3 cup sherry wine vinegar
1 cup Bing cherries, halved and pitted
3/4 cup white wine (Chardonnay)
3/4 cup red wine (Cabernet)
1 bay leaf
Salt and freshly ground pepper to taste

1. In a sauté pan with deep sides, sweat the onions in the olive oil, covered, until the onions are translucent.

2. Remove the cover of the pan and add the honey and sherry vinegar. Cook for 5 minutes, until the onions take on some color. Add the cherries, wines, and bay leaf and simmer for 15 minutes.

3. Season with salt and pepper and cook until the liquid is thickened slightly. Let cool.

Makes about 2 cups.

Compote of Dried Fruits

LONGFELLOW'S WAYSIDE INN, SUDBURY, MASSACHUSETTS

*When Henry Wadsworth Longfellow's **Tales of a Wayside Inn** was published in 1863, the tavern now known as the Wayside Inn had been in operation for nearly 150 years. The spirit of hospitality begun in 1716 by David How and his wife, Hepzibah, and ensured by the Wayside Inn Trust created by Henry Ford in 1946, remains strong today, and the inn is noted for its regional fare. This compote is customarily served with roasted pork loin glazed with maple syrup and Bourbon.*

1 cup raisins
1/4 cup golden raisins
3 cups dried apricots
1/4 cup diced dried papaya
1/4 cup dried pineapple
1/4 cup dried currants
1 tablespoon chopped fresh parsley
1/4 cup Bourbon whiskey
1/8 teaspoon cayenne pepper
3/4 cup apple cider
3/4 cup light brown sugar
Pinch of salt and white pepper

1. Combine all the ingredients in a large bowl and let soak overnight, refrigerated.

2. Heat in a sauté pan for 10 to 15 minutes and serve warm.

Makes about 5 cups.

Brandied Pear Butter

LA CORSETTE MAISON INN, NEWTON, IOWA

At La Corsette Maison, Pear Butter is a seasonal specialty, made in fall and winter and kept on hand in the freezer. It makes homemade hot breads even more delicious.

7 pears, peeled, quartered, and cored
2 tablespoons finely chopped peeled fresh ginger root
2 pounds butter, at room temperature
1 tablespoon ground cinnamon
2 cups confectioners' sugar
2 tablespoons brandy

1. Place the pears and ginger root in the bowl of a food processor and process until puréed. Remove to a bowl.

2. Place the butter in the food processor and process until smooth. Add the cinnamon, confectioners' sugar, and brandy and process until smooth.

3. With the motor running, pour the pear purée through the feed tube and process until incorporated.

Makes about 5 cups.

Liz's Pear Preserves

1810 WEST INN, THOMSON, GEORGIA

At 1810 West Inn, what is billed as a continental breakfast can include individual quiches, small pastry-wrapped sausages, and biscuits with homemade preserves. The most colorful way of presenting this recipe is to use innkeeper Virginia White's language. She advises that the preserves will be firmer if the pears are not too ripe.

A 5-gallon bucket filled with pears from our backyard pear trees
5 pounds of sugar

1. Peel, core, and slice the pears. Place in a large heavy pot with the sugar. Let sit overnight.

2. The next day, cook the mixture in the same pot over very low heat, stirring frequently, for at least 6 hours.

3. While hot, pack into hot sterile jars and seal.

Makes 8 to 10 pints.

Rosé Punch

BEAUMONT INN, HARRODSBURG, KENTUCKY

"A commodious inn admirably adapted to the demands of those seeking rest and quiet in a refined Southern environment. Stop and be refreshed." So ends the introduction to the cookbook compiled by Mary E. and Thomas C. Dedman, Jr., current owners of Beaumont Inn, which is managed by their son Charles M. Dedman, and his wife, Helen. Four generations of Dedmans have overseen the grand house (once a college for young ladies) and various outbuildings that comprise the inn. The parlors are often the scene of wedding receptions and other festive gatherings, at which punches and other libations accompany the delicious regional specialties prepared in the inn's kitchen.

2 bottles (4/5 quart each) rosé wine, chilled
1/2 cup fresh lemon juice, chilled
1/2 cup grenadine syrup, chilled
1 quart ginger ale, chilled

In a punch bowl, stir together the wine, lemon juice, and syrup. Just before serving, add the ginger ale.

Makes 3 quarts.

Lib's Almond Punch

HEMLOCK INN, BRYSON CITY, NORTH CAROLINA

From a rocker on the front porch of this informal, unpretentious inn, one looks across three valleys to the Great Smoky Mountains. The national park is just three miles away, and favorite pastimes for guests are hiking and enjoying the flora and fauna of the mountains.

6 cups pineapple juice, chilled
1 quart ginger ale, chilled
1 tablespoon almond flavoring
1/2 cup sugar

Combine all the ingredients and serve cold.

Serves 12.

Avocado Dill Dressing

WHITEHALL INN, CAMDEN, MAINE

Camden is the quintessential coastal Maine village, and since 1901 the porch of the Whitehall Inn has been a favorite spot from which to enjoy the charming town and magnificent waterfront. The Dewing family have been innkeepers here for more than twenty years, maintaining the old-fashioned friendliness and hospitality for which this popular summer hotel has been noted.

6 ripe avocados, peeled, pitted, and mashed well

1/2 cup mayonnaise

1/2 cup sour cream

1 tablespoon dill weed

1/2 tablespoon minced garlic

Pinch of salt and freshly ground pepper

Juice of 1/2 lemon

1/2 cup buttermilk, to thin

Dill pickle juice, to thin

Combine all the ingredients except the dill pickle juice and whisk to blend well. Add dill juice gradually, if needed, to achieve the desired consistency.

Makes about 2 cups.

Branded Onion Vinaigrette

THE GALISTEO INN, GALISTEO, NEW MEXICO

At first glance there seems to be a typo in the title of this recipe. But, no, in true Wild West fashion, the onion is virtually branded before being combined with the other ingredients. This is the most commonly requested salad dressing at the Galisteo Inn; everyone loves it, and it's fun to make.

1 red onion, peeled and cut in half
1/4 cup Champagne vinegar
2 tablespoons honey
1/2 tablespoon minced garlic
1/2 tablespoon Creole mustard
1 tablespoon salt
1 teaspoon freshly ground pepper
3/4 cup canola oil
1/4 cup olive oil

1. Heat an iron skillet over high heat until very hot. Lay the onion halves cut side down in the skillet and cook over high heat until they are darkly charred on the outside and semisoft inside. Remove from the skillet and roughly chop. Set aside.

2. Place the Champagne vinegar, honey, garlic, mustard, salt, and pepper in a blender and blend on low to combine. Add the onion and oils and pulse until the ingredients are combined and the onion is in medium-small chunks.

3. Let the dressing sit for about an hour before using, to allow the flavors to meld. Correct the seasoning if necessary.

Makes 1 1/2 cups.

Country Ham Salad

BEAUMONT INN, HARRODSBURG, KENTUCKY

At Beaumont, the country hams are cured with salt and hickory smoke and then hung for two years in the inn's own ham house. This tasty spread is a wonderful way to use the scraps left from preparing the many ham dishes on the menu— it can be used for sandwiches, tea sandwiches, or as an hors d'oeuvre spread.

1 cup chopped country ham

3/4 cup chopped sweet pickle

2/3 cup diced celery

1/4 cup grated onion

1/2 cup best quality mayonnaise

1/2 teaspoon sugar

1. Combine the first five ingredients and mix well.

2. Sprinkle the sugar evenly over the mixture and mix well again.

Makes about 2 cups.

Tomato, Cheese, and Pesto Croûtons

WALDEN INN, GREENCASTLE, INDIANA

These savory wedges are excellent with soups and salads and can be used as an afternoon tea or hors d'oeuvre offering as well.

2 English muffins, split

2 tablespoons crumbled goat cheese

2 teaspoons pesto

1 tablespoon chopped sun-dried tomatoes (packed in oil and drained)

1/2 fresh tomato, chopped

1 tablespoon minced scallions

1. Preheat the oven to 350 degrees F.

2. Toast the muffin halves.

3. Combine the goat cheese, pesto, sun-dried tomato, fresh tomato, and scallions and mix well.

4. Spread the muffin halves with the topping, place on a baking sheet, and bake for 10 minutes or until the topping is bubbly. Cut each half into four wedges.

Makes 16 croûtons.

The Inns and Their Recipes

The Inns and Their Addresses

UPPER NEW ENGLAND

Maine

The Captain Lord Mansion
P.O. Box 800
Kennebunkport, ME 04046-0800
207-967-3141

Dockside Guest Quarters
P.O. Box 205
York, ME 03909
207-363-2868
800-270-1977

The Inn at Harbor Head
Box 1180
Kennebunkport, ME 04046
207-967-5564

Pilgrim's Inn
Deer Isle, ME 04627
207-348-6615

The Squire Tarbox Inn
RR 2, Box 620
Wiscasset, ME 04578
207-882-7693

The Waterford Inne
Box 149
Waterford, ME 04088
207-583-4037

Whitehall Inn
52 High St.
Camden, ME 04843
207-236-3391
800-789-6565

New Hampshire

The Hancock Inn
Main St.
Hancock, NH 03449
603-525-3318
800-525-1789

The Inn at Thorn Hill
Thorn Hill Rd., Box A
Jackson, NH 03846
603-383-4242
800-289-8990

Philbrook Farm Inn
881 North Rd.
Shelburne, NH 03581
603-466-3831

Rockhouse Mountain Farm-Inn
P.O. Box 90
Eaton Center, NH 03832
603-447-2880

Staffords-in-the-Field
P.O. Box 270
Chocorua, NH 03817
603-323-7766

Vermont

Barrows House
Rte. 30
Dorset, VT 05251
802-867-4455
800-639-1620

Beaver Pond Farm Inn
RD Box 306, Golf Course Rd.
Warren, VT 05674
802-583-2861

Cobble House Inn
P.O. Box 49
Gaysville, VT 05246
802-234-5458

Four Columns Inn
P.O. Box 278
Newfane, VT 05345
802-365-7713
800-787-6633

The Inn at Montpelier
147 Main St.
Montpelier, VT 05602
802-223-2727

The Inn on the Common
P.O. Box 75
Craftsbury Common, VT 05827
800-521-2233

Juniper Hill Inn
Box 79
Windsor, VT 05089-9703
802-674-5273
800-359-2541

North Hero House
North Hero, VT 05474
802-372-8237

The Old Tavern at Grafton
Main St.
Grafton, VT 05146
802-843-2231

Rowell's Inn
RR 1, Box 267D
Chester, VT 05143
802-875-3658

Swift House Inn
25 Stewart Lane
Middlebury, VT 05753
802-388-9925

The Vermont Inn
Rte. 4
Killington, VT 05751
802-775-0708
800-541-7795

Windham Hill Inn
West Townshend, VT 05359
802-874-4080

SOUTHERN NEW ENGLAND

Connecticut

The Griswold Inn
36 Main St.
Essex, CT 06426
203-767-1776

The Homestead Inn
420 Field Point Rd.
Greenwich, CT 06830
203-869-7500

Under Mountain Inn
482 Under Mountain Road
Salisbury, CT 06068
203-435-0242

The White Hart
P.O. Box 385
Salisbury, CT 06068
203-435-0030
800-832-0041

Massachusetts

Blantyre
P.O. Box 995
16 Blantyre Rd.
Lenox, MA 01240
413-637-3556 (summer)
413-298-3806 (winter)

The Captain's House Inn
369 Old Harbor Road
Chatham, MA 02633
508-945-0127
800-315-0728

The Charlotte Inn (l'étoile)
P.O. Box 2040
Edgartown, MA 02539
508-627-4751 (inn)
508-627-5187 (restaurant)

Hawthorne Inn
462 Lexington Rd.
Concord, MA 01742
508-369-5610

Longfellow's Wayside Inn
Wayside Inn Rd.
Sudbury, MA 01776
508-443-1776

The Red Lion Inn
Main St.
Stockbridge, MA 01262
413-298-5545

The Village Inn
P.O. Box 1810
16 Church St.
Lenox, MA 01240
413-637-0020
800-253-0917

The Wauwinet
P.O. Box 2580
Nantucket, MA 02584
508-228-0145

Rhode Island

The 1661 Inn and Hotel Manisses
Spring St.
Block Island, RI 02807
401-466-2063

Nathaniel Porter Inn
125 Water St.
Warren, RI 02885
401-245-6622

MID-ATLANTIC

New Jersey

Angel of the Sea Bed and Breakfast
5 Trenton Ave.
Cape May, NJ 08204
609-884-3369
800-881-3965

The Doctors Inn at Kings Grant
2 North Main St.
Cape May Court House, NJ 08210
609-463-9330

The Mainstay Inn
635 Columbia Ave.
Cape May, NJ 08204
609-884-8690

Sea Crest by the Sea
19 Tuttle Ave.
Spring Lake, NJ 07762
908-449-9031
800-803-9031

New York

Asa Ransom House
10529 Main St.
Clarence, NY 14031
716-759-2315

Beekman Arms
Route 9
Rhinebeck, NY 12572
914-876-7077

The Bird & Bottle Inn
R. 2, Box 129
Garrison, NY 10524
914-424-3000

Friends Lake Inn
Friends Lake Road
Chestertown, NY 12817
518-494-4751

Greenville Arms 1889 Inn
P.O. Box 659
Greenville, NY 12083-0659
518-966-5219

Lake Placid Lodge
Whiteface Inn Road
Lake Placid, NY 12946
518-523-2700

The Lodge at Lake Clear
P.O. Box 46
Lake Clear, NY 12945
518-891-1489
800-442-2356

The 1770 House
143 Main St.
East Hampton, NY 11937
516-324-1770

Sherwood Inn
26 West Genesee St.
Skaneateles, NY 13152
315-685-3405

Three Village Inn
150 Main St.
Stony Brook, NY 11790
516-751-0555

Pennsylvania

Eagles Mere Inn
P.O. Box 356
Eagles Mere, PA 17731
717-525-3273
800-426-3273

Hickory Bridge Farm
96 Hickory Bridge Rd.
Orrtanna, PA 17353
717-642-5261

The Inn at Starlight Lake
P.O. Box 27
Starlight, PA 18461
717-798-2519
800-248-2519

Delaware

The Corner Cupboard Inn
50 Park Ave.
Rehoboth Beach, DE 19971
302-227-8553

Maryland

Robert Morris Inn
P.O. Box 70
Oxford, MD 21654
410-226-5111

Turning Point Inn
3406 Urbana Pike
Frederick, MD 21701
301-874-2421
301-831-8232

SOUTH

Florida

Clewiston Inn
108 Royal Palm Ave.
Clewiston, FL 33440
813-983-8151
800-749-4466

Georgia

1810 West Inn
254 North Seymour Dr.
Thomson, GA 30824
706-595-3156
800-515-1810

North Carolina

Hemlock Inn
Bryson City, NC 28713
704-488-2885

The Orchard Inn
P.O. Box 725
Saluda, NC 28773
704-749-5471
800-581-3800

Pine Crest Inn
200 Pine Crest Lane
Tryon, NC 28782
704-859-9135
800-633-3001

MIDWEST

Indiana

The Checkerberry Inn
62644 County Road 37
Goshen, IN 46526
219-642-4445

Walden Inn
2 Seminary Square, P.O. Box 490
Greencastle, IN 46135-0490
317-653-2761
800-225-8655

Creekwood Inn
(The American Grill)
Rte. 2035 at I-94
Michigan City, IN 46360
219-874-4603

Iowa

La Corsette Maison Inn
629 First Ave. East
Newton, IA 50208
515-792-6833

Kentucky

Beaumont Inn
638 Beaumont Inn Dr.
Harrodsburg, KY 40330
606-734-3381
800-352-3992

Boone Tavern Hotel
CPO 2345, Berea College
Berea, KY 40404
606-486-9358
800-366-9358

Michigan

Montague Inn
1581 South Washington Ave.
Saginaw, MI 48601
517-752-3939

Stafford's Bay View Inn
613 Woodland Ave.
Petoskey, MI 49770
616-347-2771
800-456-1917

Wickwood Inn
510 Butler St.
Saugatuck, MI 49453-1019
616-857-1465

Minnesota

Lowell Inn
102 N. Second St.
Stillwater, MN 55082
612-439-1100

Schumacher's New Prague Hotel
212 W. Main St.
New Prague, MN 56071
612-758-2133

Ohio

Murphin Ridge Inn
750 Murphin Ridge Rd.
West Union, OH 45693
513-544-2263

Wisconsin

The White Gull Inn
P.O. Box 160
Fish Creek, WI 54212
414-868-3517

WEST

Arizona

Rancho de los Caballeros
1551 S. Vulture Mine Rd.
Wickenburg, AZ 85390
602-684-5484

California

The Grey Whale Inn
615 N. Main St.
Fort Bragg, CA 95437
707-964-0640
800-382-7244

Harbor House
P.O. Box 369
Elk, CA 95432
707-877-3203

Vintners Inn
4350 Barnes Rd.
Santa Rosa, CA 95403
707-575-7350
800-421-2584

New Mexico

The Galisteo Inn
HC 75 - Box 4
Galisteo, NM 87540
505-466-4000

Grant Corner Inn
122 Grant Ave.
Santa Fe, NM 87501
505-983-6678

Oregon

Cowslip's Belle Bed & Breakfast
159 N. Main St.
Ashland, OR 97520
503-488-2901
800-888-6819

Wyoming

Wildflower Inn
PO Box 3724
Jackson 83001
307-733-4710

CANADA

Quebec

Auberge Handfield
555 boul. Richelieu
St. Marc-sur-Richelieu, Quebec
JOL 2EO
Canada
514-584-2226
800-667-1087

Hovey Manc ·
575 chemin Hovey
P.O. Box 60
North Hatley, Quebec JOB 2CO
Canada
819-842-2421
800-661-2421

Ontario

Ste. Anne's Country Inn and Spa
R.R. 1
Grafton, Ontario KOK 2GO
Canada
905-349-2493
800-263-2663

British Columbia

Hastings House Country Inn
160 Upper Ganges Rd.
Salt Spring Island
British Columbia V8K 2S2
Canada
604-537-2362
800-661-9255

Index

About the Author

LINDA GLICK CONWAY is the author of
The New Carry-out Cuisine (with Phyllis Méras),
Café Cuisine, and **Party Receipts from the Charleston
Junior League**. In addition, she was the editor for the Culinary
Institute of America's textbook, **The New Professional Chef**.
She and her husband live in Williamstown, Massachusetts.